CYRUS

MAKERS OF HISTORY SERIES

THE MAKERS OF HISTORY SERIES *includes:*

Nero
Alexander the Great
Hannibal
Julius Caesar
Cyrus
Cleopatra
Alfred the Great
William the Conqueror
Xerxes
Elizabeth I

CYRUS

MAKERS OF HISTORY SERIES
BY
JACOB ABBOTT

CANON PRESS
MOSCOW 2017

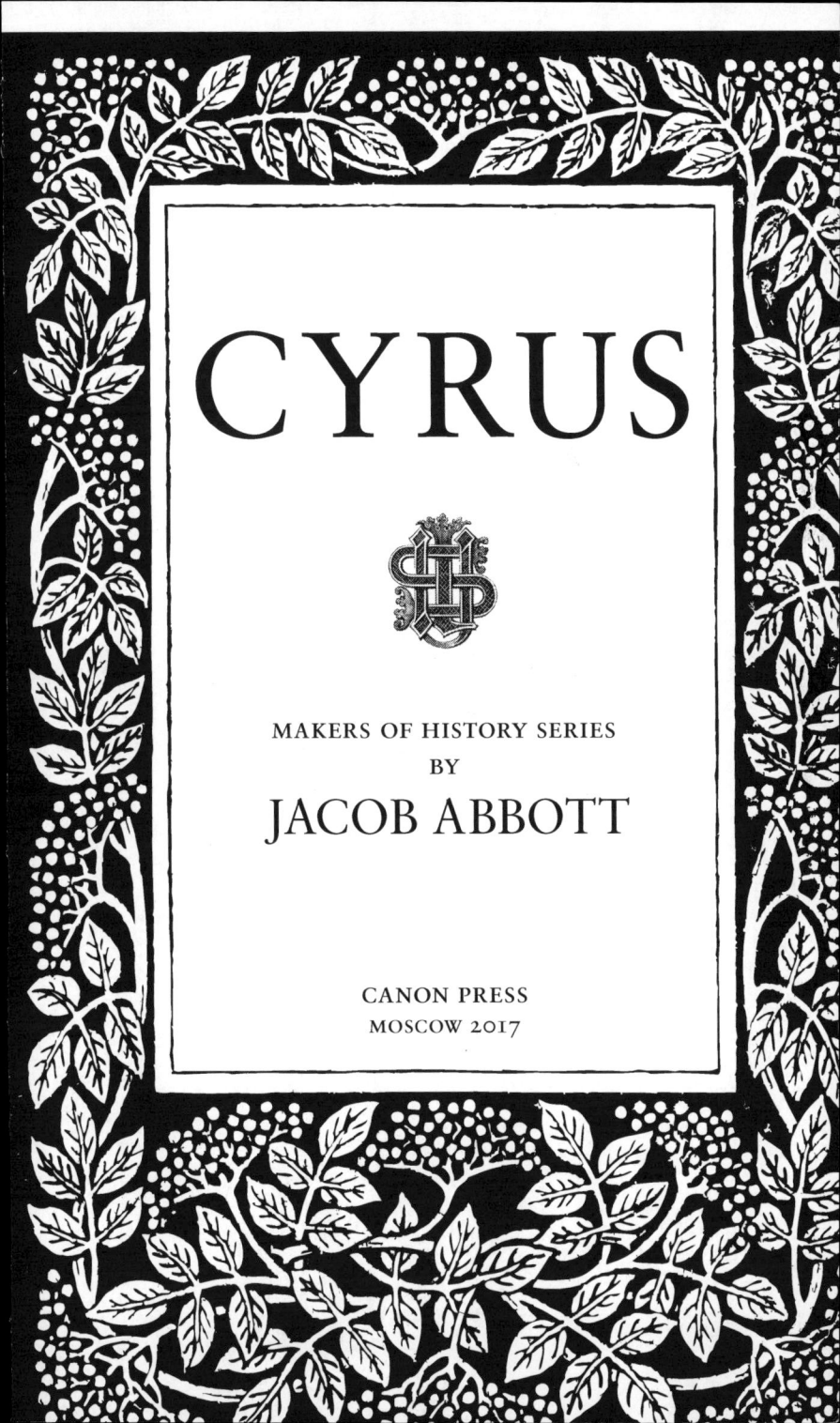

Published in the year 2017 by
CANON PRESS
P.O. Box 8729, Moscow, ID 83843
800.488.2034 | www.canonpress.com

Cyrus by JACOB ABBOTT.
First printed in 1850.
Cover design by RACHEL HOFFMANN.
Cover photoshoppery by DAVID DALBEY.
Interior design by LAURA STORM.
Updated for the present day reader by
KNOX MERKLE.
Copyright © 2017 by CANON PRESS.

The "IHS" Christogram on the title page is an ancient
symbol used in the early Western church and is derived from the first
three letters of Jesus' name in the Greek alphabet. The first use of "IHS"
in an English document was in 1377, in a printing
of the medieval classic, *Piers Plowman*.

Printed in the United States of America.
All rights reserved. No part of this publication may be
reproduced, stored in a retrieval system, or transmitted in any form by
any means, electronic, mechanical, photocopy, recording, or otherwise,
without prior permission of the author, except
as provided by USA copyright law.

Library of Congress Cataloging-in-Publication Data is forthcoming.

17 18 19 20   10 9 8 7 6 5 4 3 2 1

CONTENTS.

CHAPTER		PAGE
I.	HERODOTUS AND XENOPHON	7
II.	THE BIRTH OF CYRUS	15
III.	THE VISIT TO MEDIA	27
IV.	CROESUS	39
V.	ACCESSION OF CYRUS TO THE THRONE	49
VI.	THE ORACLES	57
VII.	THE CONQUEST OF LYDIA	65
VIII.	THE CONQUEST OF BABYLON	75
IX.	THE RESTORATION OF THE JEWS	85
X.	THE STORY OF PANTHEA	93
XI.	CONVERSATIONS	103
XII.	THE DEATH OF CYRUS	113

CHAPTER I

HERODOTUS AND XENOPHON.

CYRUS was the founder of the ancient Persian Empire, perhaps the wealthiest the world has ever seen. This empire is an extraordinary example of that strange part of human nature which causes men to keep a royal family in total power over themselves for centuries, submit to endless humiliations on their behalf, and commit the most atrocious crimes at their command.

The Persian Empire was founded in western Asia between the Persian Gulf and the Caspian Sea, five hundred years before Christ. It grew for many centuries before Cyrus became ruler and made the kingdom so famous that mankind gave him credit for its entire creation.

At the same time as this Persian monarchy was rising in the East, the small but strong republics of Greece were flourishing in the West. The Greeks had an alphabet that was easy to learn and to write, while the Persians' written language was very slow and difficult and only used by the priests for government records. The result was that the Greek writers became the historians of their own countries as well as the nations around them, because of how well they wrote about the great events of their day. Scholars have read their exciting histories for over two thousand years, and it is for this reason that the Greek language has survived.

Most of our knowledge of Cyrus and the Persian Empire comes from two of these Greek historians, named Herodotus and Xenophon. Herodotus was a philosopher and scholar who spent his life in study and travel, while Xenophon was a great general who gained fame in distant military expeditions. They were both born to wealthy families, both held high positions in society, and both led daring careers that made them famous while they were still alive. But despite these similarities, these two men wrote two very different, often conflicting accounts of the life Cyrus.

Herodotus was born in the city of Halicarnassus on the shores of the Aegean Sea in 484 BC, about fifty years after the death of Cyrus. He became a student at a very early age. In other nations, the education of young men from important families was limited to the use of weapons and horses and other skills that would make them good warriors. The Greeks, however, also taught reading, writing, poetry, history, and oratory. As a result, a general taste for intelligent pursuits spread through their communities. Public affairs were discussed before large audiences. Tragedies, poems, and songs were considered an essential part of public entertainment because the people had learned from infancy to appreciate and enjoy them.

These literary exhibitions seem to have inspired Herodotus with a great desire for knowledge and discoveries which he could share with his countrymen in these great public assemblies. Accordingly, as soon as he was old enough, he set out upon a journey through foreign countries in order to bring back a report of everything he should see and hear.

In those days, almost all knowledge of other nations was limited to the reports of the merchants whose ships and caravans travelled back and forth around the Mediterranean Sea. Occasionally, the commander of a military expedition would write a description of the countries he passed through. These accounts were more clear and reliable than those of the merchants, but the information from these two sources put together often raised more questions than it answered. Herodotus, therefore, set about to explore all the countries on the Mediterranean and in central Asia, examine their geographical position, learn their history and customs, and write it all down for the entertainment and instruction of the Greeks.

He went to Egypt first. Only recently had Egypt begun allowing travelers from other countries to visit, and Herodotus was the first to take advantage of this opportunity. While there, he took many notes of what he saw and what he thought his countrymen would like to know. From Egypt he went west into Libya, and then travelled slowly along the southern shore of the Mediterranean Sea as far as the Straits of Gibraltar, learning as much as he could and noting it all with great care.

The Straits of Gibraltar were believed to be the western end of the world in those days, and so Herodotus returned east after reaching them. He visited Tyre and Phoenicia on the eastern coast of the Mediterranean, and then continued east to Assyria and Babylon, where he learned all that he has written about the Medes, Persians, and the history of Cyrus. He then went even further east by land into the heart of Asia. The country Scythia was considered the eastern end of the world, and so after exploring this land, he turned north and then west and came down through Epirus and Macedon back into Greece. He had explored almost the whole known world.

Herodotus is widely known as the Father of History, and many see the level of detail in his writing as a sign that he only described what he actually saw. Others believe that he drew more on his imagination than any other source and never even visited half the countries he claims to have seen. This group maintains that the Father of Lies would be a more appropriate title.

Of course, often in strong controversies of this kind, the truth lies somewhere in between the two sides. Cicero says that Herodotus was the first to beautify a historical narrative, and while there is a fine line between beautifying and embellishing, it seems likely that Herodotus' writings are mostly true, though highly colored and adorned in parts. His goal was, after all, to read them in front of a large audience of Greeks, and he was likely to make them as interesting as possible.

As a result of political turmoil in his home state, Herodotus was forced to go into exile on the island of Samos, where he lived alone while he wrote out his history. He divided it into nine books, which he later named after the nine Muses. The island of Samos is very near to Patmos, where John the Evangelist wrote the Book of Revelation in the same language a few hundred years later, while also in exile.

After completing the first few books of his history, Herodotus went with the manuscript to the celebration of the 81st Olympiad. The Olympiads were events used to mark the passing of four years. These helped the Greeks keep track of time. They were celebrated with magnificent games, shows, and parades which vast crowds assembled from every part of Greece to witness and participate in. These celebrations were held at Olympia, a city in western Greece of which now only ruins are left.

Herodotus was already famous for his travels when he arrived at Olympia, and he found huge assemblies excited to hear him read large portions of his writings. Nearly all the politicians, generals, philosophers, and scholars of Greece were gathered there, and when they all applauded him, Herodotus' fame immediately grew to universal renown. Gratified at the interest his countrymen showed in his work, he at once resolved to devote all his time to completing it.

It took him twelve years to achieve this goal. He then returned to Athens during a grand festival and chose many stories to read that would be exciting to his Greek hearers—highly complimentary stories about Greek heroes and wars. The Athenians loved these tales about their ancestors' exploits. After receiving more applause than he ever had before, Herodotus was proclaimed a national benefactor and given a large public gift of money. Herodotus continued to enjoy this fame for his writing throughout the rest of his life—fame which has only been increased by the passing of time.

Because Xenophon, the other Greek historian who wrote about Cyrus, was a military commander, his life was spent very differently from Herodotus'. He was born in Athens, about thirty years after Herodotus, which meant that he was only a child while Herodotus was writing. When he was about twenty-two, he joined a military expedition to Asia Minor in order to enter the service of the ruler of that country. This ruler is known as Cyrus the Younger, in order to distinguish him from Cyrus the Great, who had lived one hundred and fifty years earlier and who this book is about.

This expedition was led by a general named Clearchus. The soldiers and officers did not know that Cyrus the Younger planned to use them to capture the throne of Persia from his brother and king, Artaxexes. Even though Cyrus was a young man, he was very ambitious and hated being ruled by his older brother. His mother encouraged his ambition, but when Cyrus attempted to assassinate his brother on the day of his coronation, Artaxerxes mercifully sent him to rule Asia Minor instead of punishing him for treason. Cyrus immediately began plotting how to take possession of his brother's throne in Babylon. Pretending to be afraid of a nearby country, he wrote to Artaxerxes, asking for soldiers, so that Artaxerxes did not suspect that the army Cyrus was building was intended to march on Babylon instead.

The army which came from Greece at this time to serve Cyrus consisted of about thirteen thousand men. Cyrus already had a hundred thousand soldiers, but the Greek warriors were so famous for their courage and their discipline, that Cyrus rightly considered them the pride of his army. Xenophon was one of the younger Greek generals. As they crossed the Hellespont and entered Asia Minor, they learned that Cyrus was going to use them to make war upon the king of Persia and so, with their suspicions confirmed, they refused to go any further—not because of any reluctance to help an ungrateful traitor destroy his own brother and benefactor, but because they felt they deserved extra pay since the work was so hazardous. Cyrus agreed, and the army went on.

Artaxerxes quickly gathered the whole force of his empire—an army consisting of over a million men. The force extended so far across the plains of Babylon, that it was only at nightfall after the battle that the Greek soldiers discovered that Cyrus' whole army had been defeated and that Cyrus was dead. Only the Greeks were left and they were commanded by Artaxerxes to surrender at once.

The Greeks refused to surrender and instead fortified themselves as well as they could and prepared for a desperate defense. There were still about ten thousand of them left and the Persians were afraid to attack them, so they instead began negotiations, pretending to be friendly and offering to allow them to return to Greece. Then, luring Clearchus and the leading Greek generals to a feast, the Persians seized and murdered them, calling it an execution of rebels and traitors. As soon as the Greek camp heard this, the whole army was thrown into dismay, for they were in a hostile country surrounded by an enemy a hundred times their size, without supplies, and with two thousand miles of rugged, difficult terrain between them and their home. And if they surrendered, they knew that they would all die in slavery.

Under these circumstances, Xenophon called together the surviving officers in the camp and recommended that they elect new commanders and immediately set out on a march for Greece. This plan was adopted. He was chosen as the new commanding general, and he led the whole force safely back through countless dangers, defending themselves every step of the way against the Persian army's attempts to surround and capture them. This retreat took two hundred and fifteen days. It is considered one of the world's greatest military achievements and is known as the Retreat of the Ten Thousand. Xenophon gained double fame by this deed, for he not only led the army to safety, but he later wrote an account of the exploit and so acquired literary as well as military renown.

Some time after this, Xenophon returned again to Asia as a military commander and distinguished himself in other campaigns. He acquired a large fortune during these wars and eventually retired to a magnificent villa near Olympia, the same city where Herodotus had become famous for his histories. Here Xenophon spent the rest of his life writing historical memoirs, no doubt influenced by the success Herodotus himself had acheived. The two most important works by Xenophon that have survived to the present day are, first, his account of his expedition under Cyrus the Younger, and, second, a tale based on the history of Cyrus the Great. This second book is called the Cyropaedia. From it and from the history written by Herodotus, nearly all our knowledge of that great Persian monarch is derived.

Whether or not the stories which Herodotus and Xenophon have told us about Cyrus the Great are true is less important than you might think, for the stories have been so widely read that they have had a greater effect on the world than the events on which they are based ever did. In fact, they have become such a permanent part of the literature of mankind that the real Cyrus is now far less important than the Cyrus of Herodotus and Xenophon. The reader must understand therefore that the purpose of this book is not an exact account of Cyrus as he actually lived, but a faithful summary of his story as it has been told throughout the world for the last two thousand years, whether fictitious or real, partial or impartial, true or embellished.

CHAPTER II

THE BIRTH OF CYRUS.

WHEN Assyria, Media, and Persia first emerged in central Asia, the three nations were already closely connected. Cambyses, the ruler of Persia, married Mandane, the daughter of Astyages, the King of Media. Their son was Cyrus, and Herodotus tells the following extraordinary story regarding his birth: while Mandane was still living in Media, her father Astyages awoke one morning terrified by a dream. In his dream, a great flood had destroyed his capital and submerged a large part of the kingdom. This alone would not have been a strange dream, for the rivers in that country often flooded quite violently. What was strange was that the great flood in his vision seemed to be connected with his daughter, which Astyages took to be a sign that Mandane would cause a great disaster to befall Media. Perhaps she would have a son who would rebel against him and seize power, overwhelming him as the flood had done in his dream.

To prevent this, Astyages decided that Mandane should not be married in Media, but instead in some far-off land. He eventually chose Cambyses, the ruler of Persia, for her husband. Cambyses was very far beneath Astyages in rank and power, and Persia was not only small but very far away, and so Astyages thought that he was safe in sending his daughter to be married there.

About a year later, Astyages had another dream. He dreamed that a vine grew from his daughter and spread rapidly over the whole land. This naturally reawakened his fears that Mandane's future son would try to take the kingdom from him, especially when his soothsayers interpreted the dream to mean that Mandane would indeed have a son who would become a king.

Astyages was now seriously alarmed, and he asked his daughter to come home for a visit, secretly hoping to destroy her child as soon as it was born. She agreed, and only a few months passed before Mandane had a son. Immediately, Astyages sent for a certain officer who, he believed, was hardened and unscrupulous enough to commit any crime he was ordered to. He addressed him as follows: "I have sent for you, Harpagus, because I need you to do something very important for me and because I have complete confidence in your ability to faithfully obey my orders and complete the task yourself. If you fail to do it or attempt to put it off on others, you will suffer severely. I wish you to take Mandane's child and put him to death. You may do this in any way you please as long as you see to it yourself that the child is killed."

Harpagus replied that it was his duty to do whatever the king might command and went to fetch the child. Believing that the infant was being taken to its grandfather for a visit, the servants of Mandane dressed it in fine

The Birth of Cyrus

clothes which its mother had spent months preparing and then gave the baby to Harpagus.

As soon as he received the child, Harpagus quickly became agitated. He sent for a herdsman named Mitridates and took the child home to explain to his wife what had happened. She asked what he intended to do and he told her: "It is the son of Mandane, the king's daughter. If the king died, Mandane would succeed him and I would be in terrible danger if I had killed her son!" But he also said that he was not willing to disobey Astyages so far as to actually save the child's life, and so he intended to have the herdsman, Mitridates, take the child into the mountains with the wild beasts and birds of prey and abandon it there.

Mitridates arrived to find Harpagus and his wife speaking thus in great anxiety and distress, with the child beginning to cry at finding itself in a strange place. Harpagus told the herdsman what he wanted him to do. Just as afraid as Harpagus had been to hesitate to obey a superior's orders, whatever they might be, the herdsman accepted the child and took it back home to his hut.

It so happened that his wife, whose name was Spaco, had just given birth to a dead son while Mitridates had been away. Not knowing why he had been called away so suddenly, she had had to bear her worry for her husband in addition to her grief at the loss of her child. But her sadness now turned for a little while into astonishment and curiosity at the magnificently dressed child her husband brought home and at the remarkable story which he told her.

He said that when he first entered the house of Harpagus and saw the child lying there and heard his orders to leave it to die in the mountains, he supposed that the child belonged to one of the servants of the household. But the richness of the infant's clothes and the deep anxiety of

Harpagus and his wife seemed to contradict this, leaving Mitridates very confused. Harpagus had then sent a man part of the way back with him, and this man fully explained the situation. The child was the son of Mandane, the daughter of the king, and Astyages had ordered him killed, lest he one day try to usurp the throne.

Those who know anything about the feelings of a mother can imagine with what emotions Spaco received the little exhausted child from her husband's hand and the heartfelt pleasure with which she held him close. In an hour, it was as if she herself was the child's mother, and she began to plead with her husband for his life.

Mitridates said that the child could not possibly be saved. Harpagus had been very clear in his orders and was coming himself to see that they had been carried out. He would no doubt demand to see the body of the child in order to assure himself that it was actually dead. Spaco only became more earnest and tearful in her pleas. But Mitridates was adamant. If they tried to save the child, Harpagus would certainly find out and then they themselves would die along with the child in the end.

Spaco then suggested that they substitute her own dead child for the living one, and leave it exposed in the mountains instead. After much doubt and hesitation, the herdsman finally agreed. They took off the splendid robes of the living child and put them on the corpse, dressing Mandane's son instead in the coarse clothes of a herdsman's child. Mitridates placed his own dead son, disguised in the royal robes, in the basket in which the other had been brought and left it in the forest.

Three days passed, and the herdsman went to inform Harpagus that the child was dead and invited him to come see the body as proof. Harpagus sent a messenger back with him. Mitridates showed him the dead child and, satisfied, the messenger reported this to Harpagus, who ordered the body to be buried. The child of Mandane, who eventually received the name Cyrus, was brought up in the herdsman's hut as Spaco's own son.

Harpagus informed Astyages that his orders had been carried out and that a trusty messenger had seen the body. But the king found very little satisfaction in the knowledge, for the same fears which had led him to commit the crime now gave way to remorse for his cruelty. Mandane mourned incessantly the death of her innocent baby and deeply reproached her father for having killed it, and in the end he repented bitterly of what he had done.

The secret of the child's preservation remained concealed for about ten years. It was then discovered in the following manner: Cyrus, like Alexander, Caesar, William the Conqueror, Napoleon, and others who obtained great power over masses of men in their adult years, showed signs of his commanding nature very early in his boyhood. He always took the lead of his playmates in their sports and made them submit to his rules and decisions. Not only did the peasants' boys in the village obey him, but even when the sons of important men came to play with them, Cyrus was still the acknowledged leader. One day the son of Artembaris, an officer of King Astyages' court, came with other boys from the city to join in the peasant boys' sports. They were playing king. Herodotus says that the other boys chose Cyrus as king, but it was probably that kind of choice where subjects simply give in to a man's determined attempts to place himself on the throne.

During the game, a quarrel arose between Cyrus and the son of Artembaris. The latter would not obey and so Cyrus beat him. The officer's boy went home with many bruises and Artembaris went straight to Astyages to complain about the indignity his son had suffered at the hands of the peasant boy. He demanded that Cyrus be punished. "Is this the treatment," he asked indignantly, showing him his son's cuts and bruises, "that my boy is to receive from the son of one of your slaves?"

Astyages seemed to think that Artembaris had just cause to complain and ordered Mitridates and his son to come to him in the city. When they arrived, Cyrus entered the presence of the king with that courageous bearing which romance writers like to ascribe to boys of noble birth. Astyages was struck by his appearance and his attitude, but sternly pointed to Artembaris' injured son and asked, "Is that the way that you, a mere herdsman's boy, dare to treat the son of one of my nobles?"

The little prince looked up into his stern judge's face with an undaunted expression and said: "My lord, what I have done I am able to justify. I did punish this boy, and I had a right to do so. I was king, and he was my subject, and he would not obey me. If you think that for this I deserve punishment myself, here I am; I am ready to suffer it."

Astyages' admiration was awakened even more now at hearing such words spoken in so high a tone by a child. He remained silent for a long time. At last he told Artembaris and his son that they could go and that he would deal with the matter himself. Astyages then took the herdsman aside and asked whose boy Cyrus was and where he had found him.

Mitridates was frightened, but replied that the boy was his own son. There seems to have been something, however, in his manner that led Astyages not to believe what he said. He was convinced that there was some mystery in the boy's origin which the herdsman was withholding. And so he took on a displeased and threatening expression and ordered his guards to take Mitridates prisoner. Terrified, the herdsman immediately promised to tell Astyages the whole truth about Cyrus.

Astyages seems to have been one of those monsters created by the long use of tyrannical power, who take great satisfaction in torturing to death any victim that they can find a reason to destroy. Many men commit cruelties in sudden anger or under the influence of violent emotions, but the crimes of a tyrant are not like this, and although Astyages rejoiced to find that the child had been saved, he saw no reason not to punish the man who had saved him. After all, Harpagus had defied his will, and therefore Astyages began to calmly and deliberately plan a way to punish him.

When at length his plan was formed, he sent for Harpagus. He began by asking Harpagus how he had destroyed the child of Mandane so many years ago. Harpagus replied with the exact truth, that he had tried to find a way to fulfill his orders without directly murdering the child himself, and that he had finally employed Mitridates to expose it in the forest and to keep watch until it was dead. He had then sent a messenger to identify the dead body and take care of its burial. He solemnly promised the king that this was the truth and that the child had been killed just as he said.

With an appearance of satisfaction, the king then informed Harpagus that the child had not been destroyed after all, and told him how it had been exchanged for the dead child of Spaco and brought up in the herdsman's hut. "After he was dead, as I supposed," he said, "I bitterly regretted giving orders to kill him. I could not bear my daughter's grief. But the child is alive, and all is well; I am going to hold a grand festival for the occasion."

Astyages then requested Harpagus to send his son, who was about thirteen, to the palace to be a companion for Cyrus. Harpagus went home, trembling at the narrow escape he had just had. He called his son and sent him to the king with many instructions on how to behave. He told his wife, and she also rejoiced in the apparent end to an affair that might have been their ruin.

The sequel to the story is too horrible to be told, and yet too important to an understanding of the effects of power on human nature to be left out. Harpagus came to the grand festival and was placed in a prominent position at the table, where a variety of food was brought in and set before the guests and eaten without question. Near the end of the feast, Astyages asked Harpagus what he thought of his food. Harpagus, half terrified with a mysterious feeling of danger, said that he was pleased with it. Astyages then told him that there was plenty more and ordered servants to bring the basket in—and Harpagus saw that it contained the head, hands, and feet of his son. Astyages told him to help himself.

The most astonishing part is that Harpagus behaved as calm and cool as if nothing had happened. The king asked him if he knew what he had been eating. He said that he did and that whatever was pleasing to the will of the king was pleasing to him.

It is hard to say whether corrupt power exerts its worst effects upon those who wield it or on those who have to bear it; on its masters, or on its slaves.

After the first feelings of relief which Astyages had felt, his former uneasiness began to return that the child should one day take the throne from him. He began once again to consider whether he should not take some measures against such an event, and so he called for his soothsayers, as he had done in the case of the dream.

When the magi heard how the boy had been discovered when he behaved like a king among his playmates, they decided that Astyages no longer had any cause for concern regarding the dream.

"He has been a king," they said, "and the danger is over. It is true that he has been a monarch only in play, but that is enough to fulfill the omens of the vision. He will never reign again. You have, therefore, no further cause to fear and may send him to his parents in Persia with perfect safety."

The king took this advice, but ordered the soothsayers to maintain their watchfulness should any further omens of danger appear, and to warn him immediately. Promising to watch faithfully, they left presence of the king, who then sent for Cyrus.

It seems that Cyrus was still unaware of his true history, for when Astyages told him he was going to Persia, he said: "You will there rejoin your true parents, who are of a very different rank in life than the herdsman whom you have lived with thus far. You will make the journey with guards who will explain to you on the way there the truth of your parentage and birth. You will learn that I tried, under the influence of a bad dream, to hurt you many years ago. But all has ended well, and you can now go in peace to your real home."

As soon as the journey was prepared, Cyrus set out to Persia. His parents Cambyses and Mandane were at first speechless with surprise, and then overwhelmed with joy at seeing their long-lost child reappear from the dead in the form of this tall and handsome boy, with health, intelligence, and happiness. They smothered him with kindness, and the heart of Mandane, especially, was filled with pride and pleasure. As soon as Cyrus became settled in his new home, his parents began to arrange as complete an education as they could for him.

Xenophon's tale of the early life of Cyrus gives a detailed account of life in Cambyses' court. The sons of all the nobles and officers were educated together in the royal palace, kept busy with activities which would train them for the duties of adult life. They were not generally taught to read, since there were no books, but they were instructed in the ways of justice: the principles of right and wrong, the country's laws, and rules for settling conflicts. The boys were also trained to apply these principles to their own arguments as practice, each taking turns acting as judge among them. If they judged right, they were rewarded, and if they judged wrong, they were punished. Cyrus himself was punished on one occasion for a wrong decision. This is how it happened.

A bigger boy took the coat of a smaller boy, because it fit him better, and gave him his own smaller coat instead. The smaller boy complained, and Cyrus was asked to judge the case. After hearing the case, Cyrus decided that each boy should keep the coat that fit him best, but the teacher told him that this was an unjust decision. "When you are asked," he said, "to decide what fits best, then you should choose as you have in this case, but when you are asked to decide whose coat is whose, then you must consider whether a man should be allowed to take a thing by force from someone weaker than himself or whether the owner should have his property protected. You have decided against law and in favor of violence." Cyrus was consequently punished for his poor reasoning.

The Birth of Cyrus

The boys at the Persian court trained in many manly exercises. They learned to wrestle, to run, to use weapons, and to hunt, which they often practiced in the nearby forest and mountains. When they did, they went armed with a bow, a quiver of arrows, a shield, a small sword, and two javelins. One of these was intended to be thrown and the other kept for close combat against the wild beasts. These hunting trips were very long, and the boys became used to hard work and rough conditions. They had to make very long marches and would encounter great dangers and fights along the way, as well as hunger, thirst, and violent weather. This was considered precisely the right sort of discipline to turn the young men into good future soldiers.

As he was only twelve years old, Cyrus was not yet old enough to take part in these dangerous exercises. He was a very beautiful boy, tall and graceful, with a striking and expressive countenance. In every situation, he always spoke his mind, honestly and without any fear. He was extremely kind-hearted and friendly as well, and careful not to say or do anything to hurt those around him. In fact he was so open, warm, sincere, and self-sacrificing that he became a favorite with everyone he met and was universally admired throughout the court, and Mandane's heart overflowed with pride for her son.

CHAPTER III

THE VISIT TO MEDIA.

WHEN Cyrus was about twelve years old, if Xenophon's account is true, he was invited by his grandfather Astyages to visit Media. Astyages had received many glowing descriptions of the prince's intelligence and character and activities, and naturally felt a desire to see his grandson again.

Cyrus had been sent to Persia before he had seen the splendor of royal life in Media, for the habits of the Persians were very plain and simple. When he arrived in Media, he was very impressed with the great parades and sights and luxuries of the royal court. Astyages took great pleasure in witnessing his little grandson's admiration for these wonders. It is one of God's great provisions that we can renew our enjoyment of the world by observing it in the company of little children and seeing it anew through their eyes, once again full of wonder and magic.

This is was the result with Astyages and Cyrus. In observing his grandson, the monarch took new pleasure in many things which had long ago lost their charm for him. Cyrus, as we have already said, very freely spoke his mind about everything he saw. Of course, as a prince he had the privilege of being able to say what he liked. But he also had a great deal of common sense, so that even if he disapproved of something, he did it in a way that was so good-natured and polite that it amused all and hurt none.

Astyages was impressed by an example of the boy's tact during their very first meeting. The Persians were accustomed to dress very plainly, whereas in Media the officers and king were always very splendidly adorned. So, when Cyrus entered his grandfather's presence, he was quite dazzled at the display of expensive clothing and jewelry. Astyages wore a purple robe, richly adorned with embroidered collars, bracelets, precious stones, flowing locks of artificial hair, and makeup on his face. Cyrus stared for a few moments and then exclaimed, "Why, mother! What a handsome man my grandfather is!"

This amused the king and the others present greatly, and so Mandane asked Cyrus whether he thought his father or grandfather handsomest. Cyrus avoided answering such a question by saying that his father was the handsomest of the Persians, but his grandfather was the handsomest of the Medes. Astyages was even more pleased by this proof of his grandson's good sense then he had been by the compliment he had received, and from then on Cyrus was able to do and say whatever he liked in his grandfather's presence.

Cyrus cared very little for the fancy clothes which his grandfather gave him, and instead continued in his habits of simple dress. There was one Median pleasure however, that he enjoyed very much, and that was learning to ride on horseback. The Persians had very few horses and kept no cavalry in their armies, and so the young were not trained in the art of horsemanship. Even on their hunting excursions, they always travelled by foot, carrying their heavy loads of arms and provisions on their backs. It was therefore a new pleasure to Cyrus to mount a horse.

Horsemanship was a great art among the Medes. Their horses were beautiful and swift and had splendid saddles and bridles. Astyages gave Cyrus the best animals he could find, and the boy was very proud to work hard at mastering this new accomplishment, for once he learned to be at home in the saddle, Cyrus felt that he had quadrupled his own worth. It seemed as though the horse's courage, strength, and speed magically became his own as he galloped over the plains, or pursued deer, or raced with his companions.

The officers and servants in Astyages' palace, as well as Astyages himself, soon began to take a strong interest in the young prince. Each enjoyed explaining their different duties and was happy to teach him whatever he desired to learn. The most important attendant in the palace was the cup-bearer, who was in charge of the tables and the wine. Astyages' cup-bearer was a Sacian, and he was not as friendly with Cyrus as the others. There was nothing in his duties that he could teach the boy, and Cyrus did not like his wine. Besides, when Astyages was busy, the cup-bearer often had to keep Cyrus from entering and interrupting him.

At one of the feasts which Astyages held in the palace, Cyrus and Mandane were invited and Astyages had a great variety of fancy dishes set before Cyrus: meats, sauces, and delicacies of every kind. He thought that Cyrus would have been awed by the display of luxury, but he did not seem pleased. Astyages asked him if the feast was not better than those in Persia. Cyrus replied that he did like eating so little of so many dishes. "What do you do in Persia?" asked Astyages. "Why, in Persia," said Cyrus, "we have plain bread and meat, and eat it when we are hungry; thus we stay healthy and strong and have very little trouble." Astyages laughed and told Cyrus he could live on plain bread and meat if he liked while he remained in Media.

Cyrus asked if he could give away all of his food as he saw fit. Astyages agreed, and Cyrus began to call up the servants to the table and to distribute the costly dishes in return for their kindnesses to him. "This," he said to one, "is for you, because you teach me to ride; this," to another, "for you, because you gave me a javelin; this to you, because you serve my grandfather faithfully; and this to you, because you honor my mother." Thus he continued until he had given away all his food. But he left out the Sacian cup-bearer. Astyages asked Cyrus why he had not given anything to the Sacian, his favorite servant.

"And why," asked Cyrus, in reply, "is this Sacian such a favorite with you?"

"Have you not observed," replied Astyages, "how elegantly he pours out the wine for me, and then hands me the cup?"

The Sacian was indeed very graceful, but Cyrus replied that he could pour wine just as well, and Astyages agreed to let him try. Cyrus then took the goblet of wine and went out. In a moment, he came in again, walking grandly with an air of self-importance that imitated the Sacian so well that the whole room was amused. Cyrus approached the king and presented the cup, imitating all the ceremonies which he had seen the cup-bearer perform—except that of tasting the wine. Then he jumped into his grandfather's lap and kissed him and said to the cup-bearer, "Now, Sacian,

The Visit to Media

you are ruined. I shall get my grandfather to appoint me in your place. I can hand the wine as well as you, and without tasting it myself at all."

"But why did you not taste it?" asked Astyages. "You should have performed that part of the duty as well as the rest." It was, in fact, an essential part of the cup-bearer's duty to pour a little wine into the palm of his hand and taste it before presenting it to the king, in order to make sure it was not poisoned.

Cyrus replied that he was afraid it was poisoned. "What led you to imagine it was poisoned?" asked his grandfather. "Because," said Cyrus, "it was poisoned the other day, when you had a feast for your friends on your birthday. I could tell. It made you all crazy. You were rude and noisy and were singing and dancing in a very ridiculous manner and could not even stand up straight. So I thought that the wine must have been poisoned."

Of course, Cyrus did not seriously mean that he thought the wine had been poisoned. He was old enough to understand the effects of alcohol and surely intended his reply as a satire upon the excesses of his grandfather's court.

"But have you never seen such things before?" asked Astyages. "Does not your father ever drink wine until it makes him merry?"

"No," replied Cyrus, "indeed he does not. He drinks only when he is thirsty, and then only enough for his thirst." He then added, in a contemptuous tone, "He has no Sacian cup-bearer, either, you may depend on it."

"What is the reason, my son?" asked Mandane. "Why you dislike this Sacian so much?"

"Why, every time that I want to come and see my grandfather," replied Cyrus, "this man always stops me, and will not let me come in. I wish, grandfather, you would let me have the rule over him just for three days."

"Why, what would you do to him?" asked Astyages.

"I would treat him as he treats me now," replied Cyrus. "I would stand at the door, as he does when I want to come in, and when he was coming for his dinner, I would stop him and say, 'you cannot come in now; he is busy with some men.'"

In saying this, Cyrus imitated, in a very silly manner, the Sacian's gravity and dignity.

"Then," he continued, "when he came to supper, I would say, 'He is bathing now; you must come some other time,' or else, 'He is going to sleep and you will disturb him.' So I would torment him all the time, as he now torments me, in keeping me out when I want to come and see you."

Such conversation, half playful and half earnest, amused everyone, even though all the attention made him too talkative and he began to appear vain. Still, there was so much true kindness in his heart that his faults were overlooked, and he remained the life and soul of the all the social gatherings which took place in the palaces of the king.

Eventually, the time came for Mandane to return to Persia. Astyages suggested that she leave Cyrus in Media, to be educated there under his grandfather's oversight. Mandane replied that it would be very hard to leave Cyrus behind unless he himself wanted to stay. Astyages put the question to Cyrus. "If you stay," he said, "the Sacian shall no longer have power to keep you from coming in to see me. You shall have the use of all my horses, and when you go home you shall take as many as you wish with you. You may have all the animals in the park to hunt, and I will provide you with boys of your own age to play with, and if there is anything else you want, you will only have to ask me for it."

The pleasure of riding and hunting in the park captivated Cyrus and so he agreed to stay. He explained to his mother that it would be a great advantage to be a skilled horseman at his final return to Persia, as that would make him superior to all the Persian youths. His mother was afraid that by living too long with the Medians, her son should learn their luxurious habits and their haughty manners. But Cyrus said that Mandane need not fear; he would return to her as dutiful as ever. So it was decided that Cyrus should stay, while his mother, bidding them farewell, went back to Persia.

After his mother was gone, Cyrus endeared himself to everyone in his grandfather's court by the nobleness and generosity which he showed as he grew. He diligently studied the various skills which were considered most important, such as leaping, racing, riding, throwing the javelin, and drawing the bow. In the contests designed to test the boys on these skills, Cyrus would challenge those he knew to be better, and allow them to enjoy the pleasure of victory, while he took satisfaction in the greater practice he thus received. He would try anything, and instead of being discouraged at his mistakes and failures, he would always laugh at them and then renew his attempts with more determination than before. Thus he made rapid progress, one by one surpassing all of his companions without causing any jealousy.

It was a great amusement to him and the other boys to hunt animals in the park, especially the deer. The park was quite extensive, but the number of the animals quickly shrank because of the boys' frequent hunting. Astyages endeavored to replace them, but soon found that all the nearby sources of tame animals had been used up. Cyrus proposed that he instead go out into the forests to hunt the wild beasts.

By this time, Cyrus had grown up to be a tall and handsome young man, with enough strength and endurance to endure the fatigue of real hunting. As his body had developed, his mind and manners had also changed. The talkative cheerfulness of his childhood had disappeared and he was quickly becoming reserved, deliberate, and cautious. He no longer entertained his grandfather's company with mimicry and childish jokes. He was silent; he watched, he listened, and spoke very rarely. He no longer needed a Sacian to keep him from interrupting Astyages, but became (as Xenophon puts it) a Sacian to himself, being careful not to enter his grandfather's palace without first making sure that the king was not busy. So he and the Sacian now became great friends.

This being the case, Astyages allowed Cyrus to go with his son Cyaxares into the forest to hunt on horseback. There were guards with Cyrus, to help him in the rough parts of the country and to protect him from danger. Cyrus talked with these attendants as they rode about hunting and the various wild beasts. They told him that bears, lions, tigers, boars, and leopards must be avoided, but that stags, wild goats, wild sheep, and wild donkeys were harmless and could be hunted with safety. They also told him that steep, rocky ground was more dangerous than any beast, for careless riders were often thrown off their horses and killed.

Cyrus listened very carefully, fully meaning to follow these instructions, but soon found that the excitement of the hunt drove all thoughts of safety from his mind. When they found a stag, they all set off eagerly in pursuit, with

Cyrus at the head. Away went the stag over rough and dangerous ground. The rest of the party stopped, but Cyrus urged his horse forward with wild excitement. Coming to a chasm, the horse stumbled, throwing Cyrus from the saddle before galloping on. Though his life was for a moment in danger, Cyrus clung to the horse's mane and pulled himself back into the saddle. His guards were terrified, though he seemed only excited, for he pursued the stag with new energy and killed him with his javelin. Then he stood and waited proudly for the rest of the party.

When his attendants arrived, however, they only scolded him for his recklessness. He had entirely disregarded their instructions, and they threatened to report him to his grandfather. Cyrus felt guilty, thinking of his grandfather's displeasure—but just at this instant, he heard more shouts. The hunting party had roused fresh game. Cyrus's returning sense of duty vanished, and he sprang to his horse and rode off toward the action. The game was a furious wild boar, and it burst from a thicket directly before Cyrus. Instead of shunning the danger, as his attendants had instructed him, he rode ahead at full speed to meet the boar and killed it with a single thrust with his javelin. Cyrus's heart was filled with even greater joy and triumph than before.

When Cyaxares arrived, he also scolded Cyrus for taking such risks. Cyrus received the rebuke quietly, and then asked Cyaxares to give him the two animals he had killed so that he could take them home to his grandfather.

"By no means," said Cyaxares. "Your grandfather would be very much displeased to know what you had done. He would not only condemn you for acting thus, but he would be severely angry with us too, for allowing you to do so."

"Let him punish me," said Cyrus, "if he wishes, after I have shown him the stag and the boar, and you may punish me too, if you think best, but please let me show them to him."

Cyaxares consented, and Cyrus arranged to have the bodies of the beasts and the bloody javelins carried home. Cyrus then presented the carcasses to his grandfather. Astyages thanked him for his presents, but said he would rather not receive gifts if it meant his grandson had to put himself in danger.

"Well, grandfather," said Cyrus, "if you do not want the meat, give it to me, and I will divide it among my friends." Astyages agreed, and Cyrus split the meat up among the boys who he used to hunt with in the park. They took their portion home, each one with a glowing account of Cyrus' valor and skill. For it was not out of generosity that Cyrus thus gave away the fruits of his labor, but out of a desire to spread his own fame.

When Cyrus was about fifteen or sixteen years old, his uncle Cyaxares was married, and to celebrate his wedding, he took a great hunting party to the frontier between Media and Assyria, where game was said to be very plentiful. Because the area was so wild, Cyaxares took a considerable force of men with him for safety, marching to the hunt like a little army. Cyrus accompanied this expedition.

When Cyaraxes reached the frontier, he decided that instead of hunting, it would be better to plunder the Assyrian territory. Xenophon explains that this was seen as a more noble enterprise because of the greater danger of fighting armed men rather than beasts and because of the greater prizes they might win. The idea that it may have been wrong to attack a neighboring nation without cause does not seem to have occurred to Cyaraxes or to Xenophon.

Cyrus distinguished himself in this expedition as he had done on the hunting trip, and when the marriage party returned home with their loot, stories of Cyrus's deeds went to Persia. Cambyses thought that if his son was beginning to take part in military campaigns, it was time for him to return home. He sent word to Media and Cyrus prepared to leave.

The day of his departure was a day of great sadness among all the members of his grandfather's palace. They travelled with him for some distance, eventually leaving him with many tears. Cyrus gave away his valuables as they left, distributing his weapons, ornaments, and costly clothing. Lastly, he gave his Median robe to a boy named Araspes, with whom he had been very close. Cyrus left these friends one by one, with a very sad and heavy heart.

The young men took these presents home, but they were so valuable that their parents sent them all back to Astyages. Astyages sent them to Persia, and Cyrus sent them all back again, with a request that Astyages give them back to those he had originally presented them to, "Which," he said, "you must do, grandfather, if you want me to ever come to Media again without shame."

Such is the story Xenophon tells of Cyrus' visit to Media. With its romantic and unbelievable details, it is a good sample of the author's whole account of Cyrus' life. It is not currently believed that these and the many similar stories Xenophon has written are true history. It is more likely that Xenophon intended them to be seen as historical fiction based on fact, written to entertain the warriors of his time and to teach philosophy, morals, and warfare. There is no sense of reality about it, from beginning to end. Events and conversations always occur at just the right time and in just the right order to create the highest dramatic effect. Everyone Cyrus trusts proves good; everyone he distrusts proves bad. All his friends are generous and noble, and all his enemies treacherous and cruel. He outwits his foes with superhuman wisdom, performs incredible feats of valor, and forms the deepest friendships. All his enterprises succeed, and if there is any failure, it is only there to heighten the final and triumphant success.

This being the nature of Xenophon's tale—or rather drama—we shall, in later chapters, only add a few more scenes from it. In the meantime, we shall continue the story of Cyrus' life with the more serious and probably trustworthy Herodotus for our guide.

CHAPTER IV

CROESUS.

THE scene of our story must now be changed from Persia and Media in the east, to Asia Minor in the west, where the great Croesus, King of Lydia, was now extending his empire along the Aegean Sea. The name of Croesus is associated with boundless wealth, and there is an old proverb "as rich as Croesus," which refers to this same king of Lydia.

The country of Lydia was in the western part of Asia Minor, bordering on the Aegean Sea. Croesus himself belonged to a dynasty called the Mermnadae. The founder of this line was Gyges, who displaced the previous dynasty in a very remarkable manner. It happened like this: the last monarch of the old dynasty was named Candaules. Gyges was a servant in his household, a sort of slave, but also a close companion of his master. Candaules was a reckless and unprincipled tyrant. He had, however, a very beautiful and modest wife named Nyssia. Candaules was very proud of his queen's beauty and was always boasting about it. On one such occasion, when he had had too much to drink, he decided that he would hide Gyges in the queen's bedroom while she was undressing for the night so he could see her beauty for himself. Gyges was horrified and begged the king not to force him to wrong the queen in this way.

But Candaules insisted, and Gyges was forced to do as the king commanded. Candaules hid Gyges behind a half-opened door with strict orders to remain there until the queen had undressed, and then to sneak out, taking great care not to be seen. Gyges did as he was ordered. The beautiful queen entered, laid aside her garments, and was preparing for bed when she heard a noise behind her. It was Gyges leaving. She at once understood what had happened, but hid her indignation and spoke to Candaules in her usual tone of voice. Caundaules inwardly rejoiced that his plan had succeeded.

The next morning, Nyssia secretly sent for Gyges and informed him that she knew everything, and now either he or her husband must die. Gyges begged forgiveness, explaining that he had had no choice, but the queen had made up her mind. "The king," she said, "by his actions has turned his claim on me over to you. If you will kill him, seize his kingdom, and make me your wife, all shall be well; otherwise you must be prepared to die."

Gyges finally agreed to assassinate the king. "How will we accomplish this?" asked Gyges. "The deed," she replied, "shall be done in the same place where I was dishonored. I will let you into our room and you shall kill Candaules in his bed."

When night came, Nyssia placed Gyges behind the same door with a dagger in his hand. He waited for Nyssia's signal that Candaules was asleep, then entered and stabbed the king. He married the queen and took possession of the kingdom, and he and his successors ruled the kingdom of Lydia for many years, creating the Mermnadae dynasty, from which King Croesus descended.

The kings of this dynasty gradually extended their power over the countries around them. Croesus' father, Alyattes, waged war to the south, every year plundering the country of the Milesians, but always taking care not to harm their villages. He did not wish to drive the people away, but to encourage them to stay and tend their lands so that there might always be new flocks and provisions for him to plunder. One year, fires that were accidentally set in a field spread to a nearby town and destroyed a temple consecrated to Minerva. After this, Alyattes found only failure in all his expeditions and wars. He sent to a famous oracle to ask the reason.

"You can expect no more success," replied the oracle, "until you rebuild the temple that you have destroyed."

But how could he rebuild the temple in the enemy's country? His men could not build and defend themselves from attack at the same time. So he decided to send ambassadors to the Milesians, asking for a truce until the temple could be rebuilt.

Thrasybulus, the king of Miletus, used this opportunity to trick Alyattes into forming a permanent peace treaty. The Milesians had indeed been greatly harmed by the loss of so much of their food and supplies to Alyattes' plundering, but Thrasybulus resolved to hide this fact. When the ambassador from Alyattes was about to arrive, Thrasybulus collected all the corn, grain, and other provisions which remained in the country, and heaped them in public parts of the city. He also gave his soldiers orders to eat freely of these stores, so that when the ambassador arrived, he found the whole city feasting on heaps of provisions. The ambassador reported this to Alyattes, who then gave up all hope of subduing Miletus through famine, and immediately formed a very solemn and permanent peace treaty with Thrasybulus. To celebrate the event, he then built two temples to Minerva instead of one.

Herodotus tells how Arion, a famous singer, made a remarkable escape at sea during the reign of Alyattes, the father of Croesus. We will give the story just as Herodotus relates it and let the reader judge whether this sort of tale is true or only intended to entertain the audiences Herodotus originally read them to.

This singer, Arion, had made a tour of Sicily and southern Italy, and was now returning to Corinth with considerable wealth. He embarked in a Corinthian ship at Tarentum in Italy. Once the sailors had him at sea, they seized his gold and silver and told him he could either kill himself or jump overboard. If he killed himself on board the ship, they would give him a decent burial when they reached the shore.

Arion was at a loss what to do. Finally, he told the sailors he would throw himself into the sea—but he asked permission to sing them one last song. They agreed. He dressed himself magnificently in the rich robes he used to wear on stage, took his harp, and proceeded to sing. When he had finished, he jumped into the sea. The sailors divided his wealth and sailed on.

Instead of drowning, Arion was carried to land by a dolphin that had been charmed by his song. After landing safely at Taenarus on the southern tip of Greece, Arion journeyed straight to Corinth, where he told the king of the sailors' crime and his remarkable escape. The king did not believe him at first, but put him in prison to wait until the ship arrived. When at last it did, the king summoned the sailors and asked if they knew anything about Arion. They said that they had left him in Tarentum. Arion was then called in. His sudden appearance in the same robes in which the sailors had last seen him so terrified the criminals that they confessed and were all punished by the king. A marble statue of a man seated on a dolphin was built at Taenarus to commemorate Arion's incredible escape.

At length Alyattes died and Croesus succeeded him. Croesus extended the power and fame of the Lydian empire even farther, and for a while won all his wars. The Aegean Sea is studded with islands along the coast of Asia Minor. In those days, these islands were beautiful and densely inhabited by a people who had many ships. Their land forces were very few, but on sea, these islands were supreme.

Croesus formed a plan to conquer these islands, and began building a fleet for this purpose, though of course, his subjects were as unused to the sea as the islanders were to land. A certain philosopher visited his court at this time, one of the seven wise men of Greece. Croesus asked if he had any news. "I heard," said the philosopher, "that the inhabitants of the islands are preparing to invade your kingdom with ten thousand horses. Croesus, who believed that the philosopher was serious, was greatly pleased at the idea of the sea-farers attempting to attack him on land. "Do you not suppose," said the philosopher after a moment, "that they will be equally pleased at the idea of fighting Lydian landsmen on the ocean?"

Croesus understood the absurdity of his plan and immediately abandoned it.

Croesus acquired his famous wealth from the River Pactolus, which flowed through his kingdom. The river brought gold in grains, nuggets, and flakes from the mountains above, and the servants of Croesus gathered the sand

and washed it, leaving behind only the heavier gold. The people who lived on the river had a different explanation for the origin of the gold. They had a story that, long ago, a king named Midas had done some service for a god, who offered to grant him a wish in return. Midas asked for the power to turn whatever he touched into gold. The power was granted. But after changing many things around him to gold, he began to find that the power was inconvenient and dangerous. His clothes, his food, and even his drink were all turned to gold. About to starve in a world of treasure, he begged the god to take back the power. The god told him to go bathe in the Pactolus. Midas did so and was saved, but a great portion of the stream's sand was turned to gold in the process.

Croesus thus quickly became very wealthy and very famous. His kingdom was wide, his palaces were full of treasure, and his court was a scene of unparalleled splendor. While enjoying this magnificence, Croesus was visited by Solon, the famous Greek politician, who was travelling to observe the practices of other states. Croesus treated Solon with great honor and showed him all his treasure. At last he said to him, "You have travelled, Solon, through many countries and have studied all that you have seen. I have heard great things about your wisdom, and I should very much like to know who is the happiest person you have ever met."

Croesus had no doubt that it would be he himself.

"I think," replied Solon, after a pause, "that Tellus, an Athenian citizen, was the most fortunate and happy man I have ever known."

"Tellus, an Athenian!" repeated Croesus, surprised. "What was so remarkable about him?"

"He was a peaceful and quiet citizen of Athens," said Solon. "He lived happily under an excellent government with several virtuous children who loved and honored their parents as long as they lived. At length, near the end of his life, a war broke out and Tellus went with the army to defend his country. He aided greatly in the defeat of the enemy and fell, at last, on the field of battle. His death was lamented by his countrymen, who buried him where he fell, with great public display of honor."

Solon began to recount the domestic and social virtues of Tellus and the peaceful happiness which he enjoyed as a result. Croesus interrupted to ask who, besides Tellus, he considered the most fortunate and happy man.

After some thought, Solon named two brothers, Cleobis and Bito, who were famous for their great strength and their devotion to their mother. He told Croesus how when their mother was about to travel to a festival at a temple, the oxen for her cart did not arrive. So Cleobis and Bito took hold of the cart's poles and pulled it and their mother some miles to the temple, while the spectators cheered, and their mother's heart was filled with pride.

Croesus here interrupted again and said he was surprised that Solon should place private citizens like these men, who had no wealth, fame, or power, before a monarch like himself, who had all of these things.

"Croesus," replied Solon, "I see you now at the height of power and grandeur. You rule many nations and enjoy wealth and luxury without bound. But I cannot decide whether you are a fortunate and happy man until I know how all this will end. If we consider seventy years the average period of life, then you have a large portion yet to come, and we cannot with certainty call any man happy until his life is over."

This conversation with Solon made a deep impression on Croesus' mind, but it was not a happy impression. He hid the resentment which these unwelcome truths had awaked in him, but he began to ignore Solon, and the philosopher soon decided to leave.

Croesus had two sons. One was deaf and dumb. The other was a very promising young man named Atys. Since Atys would succeed his father as king, he received special attention and care from Croesus. Atys was unmarried, but he was old enough to command of a large body of troops and had often distinguished himself in battle. One night, the king had a dream about Atys which greatly alarmed him. He dreamed that his son would die of a wound received from an iron spear. He at once determined to do everything in his power to avert this danger. He removed Atys from the army and arranged for his marriage. He then collected all the arrows, javelins, and every other iron-pointed weapon in the palace and had them stored in a safe place, where there could be no danger of accidental injury.

About that time there appeared at Croesus' court a stranger asking for protection. He was a prince of nearby Phrygia, and his name was Adrastus. He had accidentally killed his brother, and his father had banished him, and he was now without home, friends, or money.

Croesus received him kindly. "Your family has always been friendly to me," he said, "and I am glad to return the favor. You will live in my palace, and all you need shall be given to you. Come, forget your misfortune."

Thus Croesus received the unfortunate Adrastus into his household. Some time later, messengers came from Mysia saying that an enormous wild boar had come down from the mountains and was making havoc among the flocks of the cultivated country. The messengers asked that

Croesus send his son with hunters and dogs to help them destroy the boar. Croesus immediately agreed to send the dogs and the men, but not his son. "My son," he added, "has been recently married and is too busy with other things."

But when Atys heard this, he begged his father to let him go. "What will the world think of me," said he, "if I shun those dangers and labors which other men consider it honorable to share? What will my fellow citizens think of me? What will my wife think of me? She will despise me."

Croesus then explained to his son the reason he had been so careful to keep him from danger. He told him about the dream. "It is on that account," said he, "that I am so anxious about you. You are, in fact, my only son, for your speechless brother can never be my heir."

Atys replied that he was not surprised at his father's anxiety, but maintained that his caution did not apply in this case. "You dreamed," he said, "that I should be killed by a weapon pointed with iron, but a boar has no such weapon. If the dream had said I would die by tusk or tooth, you might well keep me from going to hunt a wild beast, but iron weapons are of men, and we are not going to fight men."

The king finally consented and allowed Atys to go. He ordered Adrastus, however, to go with the expedition and watch over Atys with the utmost care.

The band of huntsmen and dogs immediately departed. Very soon, a messenger returned, breathless and terrified, bringing the news that Atys was dead and that Adrastus himself had killed him. In the excitement of the chase, when all the huntsmen were hurling javelins at the boar, Adrastus' spear had missed and struck Atys. He bled to death on the spot.

The hunters soon returned bearing the dead body of the prince, and followed by the miserable Adrastus himself, wringing his hands and crying out in despair. He begged the king to kill him at once and put an end to his agony. He had already killed his own brother, and now he had killed the son of his greatest benefactor.

Croesus, though overwhelmed with anguish, held no resentment against Adrastus after witnessing his suffering. He did his best to soothe the unhappy man's agitation, but without success. Adrastus could not be calmed. Croesus then ordered his son buried with great and solemn honors. Afterward, the whole household returned to the palace, but despite its splendor, it now only seemed grim and gloomy. That night, Adrastus went to where Atys had been buried and killed himself over the grave.

Solon was wise to say that he could not tell whether wealth and grandeur could be counted as happiness until he saw how they ended, for Croesus was plunged into extreme grief and misery for two years because of this calamity—and yet this calamity was only the beginning of his end.

CHAPTER V

ACCESSION OF CYRUS TO THE THRONE.

WHILE Croesus had been building up his reputation of splendor on his side of the River Halys (which marked the border between Lydia in the west and Persia and Assyria in the east), great changes had taken place in Cyrus' life. From being an honest and generous child, he had become a calculating and ambitious man, with the same hunger for fame and unconcern for others which always characterizes the love of power.

Though it is uncertain that what Xenophon relates of Cyrus' visit to his grandfather Astyages is meant as a true narrative of facts, it is likely that such a visit might have occurred and that similar events might have taken place. It may seem strange that a man who once wished to put his grandson to death should now treat him such kindness. But nothing is more changeable than the whims of a tyrant.

A man who is accustomed from childhood to rule those around him never learns self-control, and instead is ruled by his own emotions. It may be jealousy, revenge, paternal fondness, hate, or love—whatever he feels, he does. He heaps a favorite with kindness at one moment and demands his assassination at the next. He imagines that his infant grandchild will become his rival and orders him left in a forest to die. When the imaginary danger has passed, he amuses himself by making the same grandchild his plaything, overwhelming him with gifts only intended to please the giver. But gifts of this sort can awaken no permanent gratitude, and Cyrus grew to see Astyages as just another ruler and potential rival.

When Cyrus returned to Persia, he soon became famous for his grace, manners, and the many warlike skills he had learned in Media. He quickly gained power over the minds of all around him, and his interest passed from games, sports, and hunting to plans of war and conquest.

In the meantime, while Harpagus had shown no resentment at Astyages' punishment, he had secretly been planning his revenge for fifteen years. He was continually looking for a chance to put this revenge into action, and naturally kept his eyes on Cyrus. Astyages was always suspicious of plots against him and watched very closely everything that passed in and out of his country. Harpagus, however, managed to stay in communication with Cyrus, and made continual reports of Astyages' tyranny and of Media's defenselessness. His hope was to encourage in Cyrus the desire to one day rule both Persia and Media.

In fact, Persia was not entirely independent of Media, but was more or less connected with the government of Astyages. Cyrus' father Cambyses, the ruler of Persia, is sometimes called a king and sometimes a satrap, which is similar to a viceroy or a governor. Whatever the title, Persia was dependent on Media, and Cyrus, in his plans to rule

Media, would have seen himself as simply seeking to rise to the top of his own country's government, rather than as attempting a foreign conquest.

Harpagus saw it in the same light. Pushing his secret and dangerous plots forward both in Media and Persia, he learned who was unhappy with Astyages' rule and then proceeded to encourage their discontent. Whenever Astyages hurt a powerful subject, Harpagus always secretly took the injured man's side, quietly complaining with him about the king's oppression. At the same time, he worked diligently to spread good reports about Cyrus among all the Medes—information regarding his talents, his character, and his just and generous spirit. In this way, the power of Astyages was quickly undermined, preparing for Cyrus' rise to the throne. During all this time, moreover, Harpagus continued to act very devoted to Astyages, always attentive and flattering. He maintained a high rank at court and in the army, and Astyages relied on him as one of his most obedient servants and had no suspicion of his true plans.

At length a favorable occasion arose, as Harpagus thought, for the execution of his plan. Astyages had committed some unusual acts of tyranny and oppression, producing extensive dissatisfaction among his people. Harpagus very cautiously shared his plans to depose Astyages and put Cyrus on the throne, and found the nobles very welcoming to the idea.

The next thing was to find some secret way of communicating with Cyrus, as discovery of this plan would certainly result in Harpagus' death. He did not dare to send the message with any messenger for fear of betrayal, nor was it safe to send a letter, lest it be read by Astyages' spies. Harpagus finally adopted the following extraordinary plan: he wrote a letter to Cyrus and hid it in the body of a hare, sewing up the skin so that no signs of the incision remained. He gave this hare and some hunting gear to certain trustworthy servants, ordering them to deliver the hare into Cyrus' own hands. Harpagus felt that this would be safe, for his servants would only be seen by Astyages' spies as hunters returning with their game.

The plan was perfectly successful. The men passed into Persia without any suspicion and delivered the hare to Cyrus. He opened it and found the following letter: "It is clear, Cyrus, that you are a favorite of Heaven and that you are destined to a great and glorious career. You could not have otherwise so miraculously escaped the snares set for you in your infancy. You know by what extraordinary events you were preserved and what unusual prosperity has followed you. You also know what cruel punishments Astyages has inflicted on me for saving you. The time has now come for retribution. Persuade the Persians to revolt, put yourself at the head of an army, and march into Media. I shall probably be put in command of the army sent to stop you. If so, we will join our forces and I will enter your service. I have spoken with the leading nobles in Media, and they are ready to take your side. You will find everything prepared for you here; come therefore, without delay."

Cyrus was thrown into a fever of excitement and agitation on reading this letter, and determined to agree to Harpagus' proposal. He pondered for some time how he could raise the necessary force without openly announcing his plan. Any public action like that would immediately become known to Astyages. He determined to resort to deceit—or, as he called it, stratagem, for war always seems to justify falsehood and treachery.

Cyrus had a letter forged to look like a commission from Astyages, appointing him commander of a body of Persian soldiers to be raised for the service of the king. Cyrus read the false document in the public assembly and called upon all the Persian warriors to join him, ordering them to assemble on a certain day, each with a woodsman's ax. When they were gathered, he marched them into the forest and set them to work chopping trees and piling them up to be burned. Cyrus kept them busy with this severe toil for the whole day, giving them poor food and little rest, and only dismissing them when night had fallen. He ordered them to assemble again the next day.

On the second day, they gathered to find a great banquet waiting for them, and Cyrus directed them to spend the day feasting on rich wines and meats of all kinds. Being tired from the previous day's hard work, they were more than ready to obey. So they spent the hours in feasting, relaxing on the grass, and entertaining each other with tales, song, and dancing. At last, in the evening, Cyrus called them together and asked which day they liked best. They replied that there was nothing to like in the first day and nothing to dislike in the second.

"It is so," said Cyrus, "and you have your destiny in your own hands to spend your lives like either of these days. If you follow me, you will enjoy ease, abundance, and luxury. If you refuse, you must toil as you do now until the end of your days." He then explained to them his plans. He told them that although Media was a great and powerful kingdom, they were just as good soldiers as the Medes, and he had made arrangements that would ensure their victory.

The soldiers received this proposal with great enthusiasm. They declared themselves ready to follow Cyrus anywhere and immediately began preparing for the expedition.

Astyages soon learned of this and sent an order to Cyrus, summoning him immediately. Cyrus sent back word that Astyages would probably see him sooner than he wished, then continued with his preparations. When all was ready, the army marched across the frontier into Media.

Meanwhile, Astyages had gathered a large force and put it under the command of Harpagus, as he had expected. Harpagus told his plan of joining Cyrus to as many of his soldiers as he could trust, so that they marched to meet the invaders with part of the army set on defeating Cyrus and the other part secretly preparing to join him.

When the battle began, the honest part of the Median army fought valiantly at first, but when they found themselves betrayed and abandoned by their comrades, they were soon overpowered by the Persians. Some were taken prisoner, some fled back to Astyages, and others simply joined Cyrus' army. Cyrus, thus encouraged and strengthened, advanced toward the capital.

Astyages, when he heard of Harpagus' betrayal and his army's defeat, was thrown into a frenzy of rage and hate. The long-dreaded prediction of his dream seemed about to be fulfilled. The magi who told him that there was no longer any danger of Cyrus becoming king had either deceived him or were worthless impostors, and so Astyages ordered them all crucified.

He then ordered every man able to bear arms to report for military service, and, putting himself at the head of the immense army he had thus raised, marched to meet his enemy. He no doubt thought himself sure of victory, but he underestimated Cyrus' discipline, resolve, and terrible energy. He was defeated. His army was totally cut to pieces, and he himself was taken prisoner.

Harpagus was present when Astyages was captured, and he rejoiced in vengeful triumph over the fallen tyrant. He asked Astyages what he thought now of forcing a father to eat the flesh of his child. Astyages asked Harpagus if he thought the success of Cyrus was owing to what he had done. Harpagus replied that it was, and proudly explained the plots he had formed and the preparations which he had made, so that Astyages might see that his destruction had been caused by Harpagus alone in retribution for the terrible crime the king had committed so many years before.

Astyages told Harpagus that he was a miserable wretch, foolish for having put power into another's hands when he might have taken it himself, and wicked for having betrayed his country in order to satisfy his own private revenge.

The result of this battle was the complete overthrow of Astyages and the establishment of Cyrus on the united throne of Media and Persia. Cyrus treated his grandfather with kindness. He kept him confined, it is true, but in such cases some large and splendid residence is usually assigned to the royal prisoner, watched by troops that seem much more like a guard of honor attending a prince than jailers confining a prisoner. It was probably in such an imprisonment that Astyages passed the rest of his days. The people, tired of his cruel tyranny, rejoiced in his downfall and quickly submitted to the fairer government of Cyrus.

Astyages came to his death many years later in a remarkable way. Cyrus sent for him to come to Persia, where he himself was living. The officer who was escorting Astyages took him into a desolate wilderness, where he died of fatigue, exposure, and hunger. It was thought that this was done because of secret orders from Cyrus. The officer was cruelly punished, but it may have been only for appearances, to divert suspicion that Cyrus could have been involved in such a crime.

The whole revolution which has been described in this chapter, from its first thought to its final execution, was done in a very short period of time, and Cyrus found himself very unexpectedly and suddenly elevated to a throne.

Harpagus continued in his service, and became one of his most famous generals.

CHAPTER VI

THE ORACLES.

AS soon as Cyrus was established as King of the Medes and Persians, his power began to extend westward toward the empire of Croesus, king of Lydia. Croesus was roused from the dejection which the death of his son had caused, and began to consider how he might defend himself against Cyrus.

The River Halys, a great river in Asia Minor, was the eastern border of the Lydian empire. Croesus began to consider raising an army and crossing the Halys to invade Cyrus' own empire, rather than waiting for Cyrus to bring war to him. Still, invading Persia would be a vast undertaking, and after carefully thinking it over, Croesus found himself still uncertain what to do.

There were four or five locations in the Greek countries which, people believed, possessed supernatural power and could grant people visions of the future. The three most important of these oracles were at Delphi, Dodona, and the Oasis of Jupiter Ammon.

Delphi was a small town built in an amphitheater-shaped valley on the southern side of Mount Parnassus. Delphi was beautiful, with the mountain behind it and steep rocks descending to the flat country in front of it. These cliffs were used as walls to defend the temple and the town. In very early times a cavern was discovered in rocks, from which poured vapors which produced strange effects on those who breathed them. People went there to receive the inspiration and knowledge which they believed the vapors gave. Finally, a temple was built and a priestess lived there, sitting on a sacred three-legged stool, inhaling the vapors, and answering questions. This oracle eventually became so famous that the greatest kings would come from far away with rich gifts, hoping that Apollo, the god of the oracle, would give them positive replies.

Another of the most famous oracles was at Dodona. Dodona was northwest of Delphi on the shores of Adriatic Sea. The priestess there told Herodotus that the origin of this oracle was as follows: in ancient times, two black doves were set free in Thebes, a city in Egypt. One flew north across the Mediterranean Sea until it landed on a beech-tree at Dodona, where it said, in a human voice, that the spot had been divinely chosen to be the site of an oracle. The other dove flew west to the Oasis of Jupiter Ammon.

In the days of Herodotus, there were three priestesses at Dodona. Their names were Promenea, Timarete, and Nicandre. The answers of the oracle were, for a while, obtained by the priestess by observing how the sacred beech tree blew in the wind. In later times, the responses were got in an even stranger manner. There was a bronze statue of a man holding a whip of three lashes formed of bronze chains. These lashes hung over a great bronze cauldron in such a way that wind would blow them against its sides, causing the cauldron to ring like a gong. The sound was not loud, but it seemed supernatural, for it would continue for hours after the cauldron had been touched, no matter how gently, by the whip.

People who wished to consult this oracle came with rich presents both for the shrine and for the priestesses, who would form their answers by interpreting the mysterious sounds made by the cauldron.

The second black dove, as we have said, landed in the Oasis of Jupiter Ammon, a fertile spot in the deserts west of Egypt, about a hundred miles from the Nile. It was first discovered in the following way: a certain king was marching across the desert with his army dying of thirst when a ram appeared and led them to a long, green valley. The ram vanished and a spring of water sprang up where he had stood. The king built a sacred temple on the spot which was called the temple of Jupiter Ammon. Here the second dove alighted, and ever afterward the oracles spoken by the priests there were considered divinely inspired.

These were the three most significant oracles. There were, however, many others of less importance, all with their own unique, absurd rituals. At one there was a sort of oven-shaped cave in the rocks into which one descended by a ladder. Before consulting this oracle, the applicant had to offer many sacrifices, wash in a stream, and drink from two cups of magical water—one called the water of forgetfulness, and the other called the water of remembrance. At another of these oracles, in Attica, there was a marble statue of an ancient prophet. Whoever wished to consult the oracle would sacrifice a ram and then sleep on the ram's skin in front of the statue, receiving the oracle's answers in dreams.

Croesus wished to learn whether he could expect success if he invaded Cyrus' empire, and in order to determine which oracle was the most reliable, he devised a plan of testing them all. He dispatched messengers from Sardis, his capital, sending one to each oracle. In order to allow time for them all to arrive, he ordered them to wait one hundred days, and then ask the oracles what Croesus, king of Lydia, was doing at that moment.

He counted the days with great care, and at the appointed hour on the hundredth day, he boiled the flesh of a turtle and of a lamb together in a bronze container covered with a brass lid. He then waited as the messengers returned, one by one, all with unsatisfactory replies—except the message from the oracle at Delphi. The answer was in verse, as the responses of that oracle always were. The priestess who sat upon the three-legged stool would give her replies in a mumbled and half-intelligible manner, as impostors often do, and then attending priests would write them out in verse.

The verse which came back from Delphi was in Greek, but this will give some idea of its style and meaning:
"I number the sands, I measure the sea,
What's hidden to others is known to me.
The lamb and the turtle are simmering slow,
With brass above them and bronze below."

Croesus decided that he would rely on the oracle at Delphi for guidance in his military campaign against Cyrus. He provided the most extraordinary presents, some to be taken to the temple at Delphi and preserved as sacred gifts, and others to be burnt in sacrifice to the god. He prepared an incredible number of decorated couches, gold dishes, rich robes, and other items to be used in the ceremony leading up to his questioning of the oracle. When the time arrived, a vast crowd of people assembled to watch the animals sacrificed and feast on the meat. When this was done, the couches, goblets, utensils, robes, and everything else that had been used in the ritual was heaped into a great pile and set on fire as a sacrifice.

Other objects were presented to the temple itself, far more magnificent and costly. There was a silver cistern large enough to hold three thousand gallons of wine which was to be used in the great festivals at Delphi. There was a smaller cistern of gold. There were basins and vases and statues, all of silver and gold. The gold that was taken from the fire was recast as a lion standing on huge golden plates, and set up inside the temple.

There was one item that was somewhat more extraordinary than the rest. It was called the bread-maker. It was an image representing a woman, one of Croesus' servants, whose duty it was to bake bread. Croesus honored her with a statue of gold because she had once saved his life. Croesus' mother had died young, and his father had married a second time. The second wife wished one of her own children to replace Croesus as heir to the throne, and so she gave poison to the bread-maker to put into Croesus' bread. The bread-maker promised to obey, but instead gave the poison to the queen's own children. In gratitude, Croesus caused this statue to be made once he came to the throne, and now placed it at Delphi, to remain forever. The memory of the faithful servant was indeed immortalized, but the statue itself and all the other treasures have long since disappeared.

Croesus did not go himself to Delphi, but sent them with trusted messengers with instructions to perform the ceremonies, offer the gifts, and then approach the oracle with the follow words: "Croesus, the ruler of Lydia and various other kingdoms, has sent you these gifts. He now desires to know whether it is safe for him to march against the Persians and if he should seek the aid of any allies."

The answer was as follows: "If Croesus crosses the Halys and makes war against Persia, a mighty empire will be overthrown. It will be best for him to form an alliance with the most powerful states of Greece."

Croesus was extremely pleased with this response. He immediately resolved to begin his expedition against Cyrus. In order to show his thanks, he sent to Delphi to inquire the number of inhabitants in that city. When the answer came back, he sent a gift of money to every one of them. The Delphians in turn gave special privileges and honors to the Lydians and Croesus, including special access to the oracle.

Croesus took the opportunity to ask the oracle whether his power would ever decline. The oracle replied in a couplet of Greek verse. It was as follows:

"When a mule has made his seat upon the Median throne,
Then—and not till then—shall Croesus lose his own."

This answer also pleased the king very much. The idea of a mule reigning in Media he naturally regarded as a fancy way of describing an impossibility and so considered his power perfectly secure. He immediately began organizing his expedition and made arrangements to form the Greek alliance which the oracle had recommended. The plans he formed and the events that resulted will be described in later chapters.

It is important to note that there has been much discussion among scholars about how the oracles were able to maintain so much belief among a people as intelligent as the Greeks for so long. No doubt it was through a combination of various methods. There is a natural love of the marvelous and the supernatural in all lower classes, which makes them likely to exaggerate any extraordinary events until they seem miraculous. The cave at Delphi might really have emitted gases which affected those who breathed them. It would be easy for those who witnessed it to imagine that divine powers must exist in those gases.

The priests and priestesses, of course, had a strong interest in keeping up the belief in their reality, as their support came from the people who visited. They invented countless ways for gathering money and gifts from these visitors. In one case there was a sacred stream where people were allowed to bathe, after which they were expected to throw pieces of money into the stream. What happened to the money later is not difficult to imagine.

Nor is it necessary to believe that all these priests and priestesses were liars. Having been trained from infancy to believe that the inspirations were real, they would see them as such for the rest of their lives. Even today, if we closely examine our mental habits, we can find ourselves taking for granted many errors which we were taught as children, even if our reason and senses show them to be clearly false. Therefore, the priests and priestesses may have been as honestly deceived as anyone else.

The answers of the oracles were generally vague and open to almost any interpretation. And whenever an event even seemed to match a prediction or could be made to seem to, the story would of course spread, being improved at each repetition. Where there was failure, there would be no interest in telling the story. Therefore the cases which seemed to prove the truth of the oracle would be universally known, and the others quickly forgotten.

There is no doubt however, that in many cases the responses were arranged ahead of time by an agreement between the oracle and the one who consulted, for the purpose of fooling others. For example, let us suppose that Croesus wished to establish the believability of the Delphic oracle in order to encourage his countrymen to enlist in the army and follow him to war against Cyrus with confidence; it would have been easy for him to give the priestess at Delphi secret information that she could then use to bolster her own prophetic powers.

The fact that so many supposed revelations from Heaven have been lies is not proof that there are no true revelations at all. It is in fact strong evidence against it. God has given us no useless instincts, and the tendency of men to believe in the supernatural and seek revelations from Heaven is the strongest possible natural evidence that there really is a supernatural realm and that man may communicate with it.

CHAPTER VII

THE CONQUEST OF LYDIA.

HERE were three reasons Croesus decided to cross the Halys river and invade the empire of the Medes and Persians: first, he wanted to expand his own empire; second, he was afraid to let Cyrus attack him first; and, third, Astyages was his brother-in-law and Croesus felt obliged to help him recover his throne from Cyrus. The first thing Croesus did was form an alliance with the most powerful of the states of Greece, as he had been instructed by the oracle. After much thought, he decided that the Lacedaemonian state was the most powerful. Their chief city was Sparta, in the Peloponnesian peninsula. They were a stern, warlike people and desired nothing but military glory in return for their assistance.

Croesus sent ambassadors to Sparta to share his plans and request their aid. He told them that the oracle at Delphi had instructed him to seek an alliance with the most powerful Greek states. They were flattered by the compliment and readily agreed. Besides, they were already on friendly terms with Croesus, for he had once generously supplied them with much gold to build a statue and refused any payment in return.

Meanwhile at Sardis, Croesus continued to prepare his campaign. One of his counselors, named Sardaris, tried very hard to persuade him not to undertake this invasion. "You have nothing to gain by it if you succeed," said Sardaris, "and everything to lose if you fail. Consider what sort of people these Persians are whom you are going to war with. They live in the simplest conditions, without luxuries, without pleasures, without wealth. If you conquer their country, you will find nothing in it worth taking. And if they conquer you instead, they will enter Lydia like a vast band of plunderers. I counsel you to leave them alone and to remain on this side of the Halys."

But Croesus was not in a mood to be persuaded.

When everything was ready, the army marched eastward through Asia Minor until they reached the Halys. The army camped there on the banks, while a plan was formed for crossing the stream. Croesus was aided in this by a famous engineer called Thales of Miletus. He was an excellent mathematician, and many stories are told of the discoveries and projects which made him famous.

For example, once while travelling through Egypt, he devised a very simple way of measuring the height of the pyramids. He set up a pole and measured the length of both the pole and its shadow. He also measured the length of the pyramid's shadow. Then he calculated the height of the pyramid by using the proportion between the pole's shadow and the pole's height, and applying that to the length of the pyramid's shadow.

THE CONQUEST OF LYDIA

Thales was also an astronomer. He calculated more closely the length of the year and predicted many eclipses. In addition, he wrote several of the geometry theorems and proofs now included in the Elements of Euclid. The famous fifth proposition of the first book was his own discovery and was a much greater accomplishment than measuring the height of the pyramids by their shadow.

But to return to Croesus. Thales took on the project of transporting the army across the river. He examined the banks and found a point where the land was low and level all around. He then brought the army up to this point and had them camp as close together as possible. While they were camped, a vast number of workers dug a new channel for the river and then diverted it so that it ran behind the army. The soldiers then crossed the old, empty riverbed without difficulty.

Having passed the Halys, Croesus moved on towards Media. He did not have to go far before he met his enemy. Cyrus had heard of his plans from deserters and spies, and had been marching to meet him for some time. He brought each of the nations he passed through under his control, either through force or through treaties and alliances, and he had gathered reinforcements from all of them. Only the Babylonians remained. They were on the side of Croesus. They were jealous of the growing power of the Medes and Persians and had promised to aid Croesus in the war. The other eastern nations were allied with Cyrus, and he was slowly approaching with an immense combined force at the same time that Croesus was crossing the Halys.

The scouts ahead of Croesus' army soon brought reports of a large armed force coming to meet them. Cyrus' scouts brought back similar intelligence and two armies halted and began to prepare for battle by the plain of Pteria in Cappadocia, which is in eastern Asia Minor.

A great battle was then fought. It continued all day and only drew to a halt when darkness fell. Both kings seemed to find their opponent stronger than expected, and neither renewed the battle on the next morning.

Croesus felt himself fortunate in holding off Cyrus' formidable army. He had no doubt that Cyrus would now go back to Media, having found how well-prepared Croesus was. Croesus himself decided that he would return to Sardis to strengthen his army, as he had lost many men in the battle, and to postpone his invasion until the next year. So he set out, sending messengers to Babylon, Sparta, Egypt, and other allies, informing them of the great battle of Pteria and asking for reinforcements next spring to join his great campaign.

He continued homeward without interruption, sending troops back to their homes as they passed them on the way. By temporarily disbanding part of his army, he thus saved the expense of having to maintain them through the winter.

Very soon after Croesus arrived at Sardis, the whole country was thrown into alarm by the news that Cyrus was close at hand. It seems Cyrus had waited just long enough to allow Croesus to leave Pteria and then had marched after him toward Sardis as quickly as possible. Croesus, in fact, had no news of Cyrus' approach until he was already there.

Croesus quickly gathered all the forces he could and summoned troops from the neighboring cities to hurry to the capital. He then armed the citizens and thus collected a formidable force in a short amount of time, assembling them on a great plain not far from the city to wait for Cyrus' attack.

Since the Lydian army was superior to Cyrus' in terms of cavalry, and the battle plain was perfect for that type of force, Cyrus was a little concerned. Nothing is more terrifying than the charge of a vast squadron of cavalry, flashing their sabers and trampling everything in the dust. The only way to withstand the charge is to arrange your foot soldiers in triple rows with their spears planted against the ground, points outward. Even then, the horses soon break through the lines, leaping over those that the spears kill and soon putting their enemies to flight.

Cyrus, unfortunately, had no troops suitable for opposing Croesus' horses. He did, however, have a great number of camels which had carried their baggage and supplies and Cyrus decided to try to use them against the cavalry. It is said by ancient historians that horses cannot bear the sight or smell of a camel, although this does not seem to be true today. Regardless, Cyrus arranged his camels in front of his army as they advanced, each mounted by a soldier with a spear.

The battle began. But as soon as the squadrons of horse reached the camels, they were thrown into confusion and began to flee. Whether this was because of the horses' hatred of the camels or because of the resistance that the camel riders made, Croesus' cavalry became totally uncontrollable, and turned and trampled the foot soldiers of their own army. Croesus' army was defeated and fled back into the city in utter disarray.

Cyrus advanced, surrounding the city on all sides, and began a siege. The situation did not look promising. The walls were very tall and very thick, with more than enough people inside to guard them. Furthermore, Croesus' wealth had enabled him to store up almost inexhaustible supplies of food, and he hoped to hold out until help should come from his allies, to whom he had sent messengers.

The city of Sardis was built in a naturally strong position, and one part of the wall was built over rocky cliffs that were thought entirely impassable. This portion of the wall was poorly built and weakly guarded. There was an ancient legend that, while a man named Males was king of Lydia, one of his wives had a son that looked like a lion. They called him Leon. An oracle declared that if Leon were carried around the walls of the city, it would be made unconquerable and would never be captured. They carried Leon around the regular walls, but turned back when they came to these cliffs, believing that this part of the city was already invincible.

Cyrus continued the siege for fourteen days, and then determined that he must find some way of taking it by assault. He sent horsemen to explore the walls and offered a large reward if they could find a place where the walls could be scaled. They all returned unsuccessful. A certain soldier named Hyraeades, after studying the invincible cliffs, saw a sentinel climb down the rocks to get his helmet, which he had accidentally dropped. Hyraeades watched him descend and then climb back up. He mentioned this to others, and they began to discuss the possibility of scaling the cliff and the walls at this point. In the end, Hyraeades went up first, followed by a few more glory-seekers. They were not seen from above. Great numbers of soldiers began to follow them up, and thus so large a force snuck into the city that they were able to capture it.

During the dreadful chaos as the city was stormed, Croesus himself had a very narrow escape from death. He was saved by his deaf and dumb son, who miraculously

The Conquest of Lydia

spoke on that occasion. Or at least that is the story. Cyrus had given orders that his soldiers must not harm Croesus, but take him alive. During the battle, when the streets were filled with wild, enraged soldiers, a group of Persians overtook Croesus fleeing with his helpless son. They were about to kill Croesus with their spears when the son, who had never spoken before, called out, "It is Croesus; do not kill him." The soldiers instead took Croesus prisoner and led him away to Cyrus.

Croesus had long ago asked the Delphic oracle how the power of speech could be given to his son. The answer was that he should not ask, for the day on which his son spoke would be the darkest day of his life.

Cyrus had not ordered his soldiers to spare Croesus' life out of mercy or pity, but because he wished to decide what to do with him himself. When Croesus was brought to him, he put him in chains and had him carefully guarded. As soon as order was restored to the city, a large funeral pyre was built in the public square and Croesus was brought to the spot. Fourteen young Lydian men were brought with him, and they were all placed on the wood of the funeral pyre. Croesus watched in horror as the Persians prepared to light the pyre. His heart sank and spectators watched in solemn silence. Croesus finally broke the silence, calling out in despair, "Oh Solon! Solon! Solon!"

The officers who had charge of the execution asked him what he meant. Cyrus, who was personally overseeing the situation, also asked for an explanation. Croesus was at first too agitated to reply. There were also difficulties in language, which hindered the conversation, as the two kings could only speak through an interpreter. Croesus told the story of his conversation with Solon, and of how no one could decide if a man was truly happy until his life had ended. Cyrus was interested in this story, but the officers had already lit the fire and it was quickly burning its way through the funeral pyre. Cyrus ordered it extinguished and although the soldiers' efforts seemed in vain, there was a sudden shower of rain which put out the flames. Croesus and the captives were saved.

Cyrus immediately, with the inconstancy common to monarchs, began to treat Croesus as a friend. He ordered him to be unbound, brought forward, and treated with honor. Croesus remained with Cyrus for a long time and accompanied him in later wars. He was very angry with the oracle at Delphi for deceiving him with its false prediction. He took the shackles with which he had been chained and sent them Delphi, asking whether this betrayal was the kind of gratitude they showed to a man who had given them so many gifts.

The priests of the oracle replied that the destruction of the Lydian dynasty had been decreed by the Fates as revenge for the guilt of Gyges, the founder of the line. He had murdered his master and taken his mistress and the throne without claim. The judgments of Heaven had to fall upon Gyges or one of his descendants for this crime. Apollo at Delphi had done all he could to postpone the punishment until after Croesus' death, but the decrees of the Fates were unchangeable. All the oracle could do was warn Croesus, which it had done by telling him that crossing the Halys would cause the destruction of a mighty empire—his own. The oracle had also told him that he would lose his power when a mule sat on the throne of Media. Cyrus was the mule. He was descended from the Persians on one side and the Medians on the other, just as a mule is born from a horse and a donkey.

When Croesus heard this answer, he was satisfied and admitted that the oracle was right and he himself had been wrong. Indeed, there has always been a great tendency to overlook any injustice in the lies of the oracle, because of the cleverness which its priests always show in saving themselves from exposure as frauds.

CHAPTER VIII

THE CONQUEST OF BABYLON.

IN his march toward the lands of Croesus in Asia Minor, Cyrus had passed to the north of the great city of Babylon. Babylon was on the Euphrates River. It was the capital of a large and fertile region which ran down both sides of the Euphrates to the Persian Gulf. The limits of the land ruled by Babylon, however, varied greatly from war to war.

The River Euphrates was the great source of fertility for that whole region. The country watered by this river was very densely populated by hard-working, peaceful people. There were many canals in the land, irrigating the farms with water from the river. Some of these canals were large enough to be navigated by ships, and one in particular joined the Euphrates with the Tigris and could be sailed by large ships with great burdens.

Most of the country's traffic was, however, conducted on boats of moderate size which interested Herodotus greatly. Babylon was enormous and required immense supplies of food, which were brought down from the farms by these boats, which were built in the following way: first a broad and shallow frame was built with the front and back of exactly the same shape. This frame was made of willows, like a basket, and then covered with a layer of skins. Reeds were spread in the bottom to protect the frame and evenly distribute the pressure of the cargo. The boat was then loaded and floated down the river to Babylon. The boatmen were careful to protect the leather hull by avoiding any contact with rocks or even the gravel on the shore. They steered their boats down the middle of the river with two oars, one at the front and one at the back.

These boats were usually fairly large and often carried donkeys or mules in addition to their cargo and crew. When the boats arrived at Babylon, the cargo was sold, the boats were taken apart, and the leather skins were packed up for the mules to carry back up the river with the boatmen to be used to build more boats for the next voyage.

If the accounts are true, Babylon was four or five times as large as London, although much of this space held open squares and royal parks and gardens. Also, houses in those days were much lower to the ground and so took up more space. The walls of the city are described by some as seventy-five feet high and by others as two or three hundred feet high. There has been much debate regarding these statements and many attempts to reconcile them, but it is not surprising that there should be so much difference in the recorded measurements, for the walls of an ancient city were rarely the same height all the way around. They varied according to the ground they were built on. Where the ground would give attackers an advantage, the walls had to be high. Where the ground itself provided some defense, the walls could be lower. So it is entirely possible that in certain places, such as over ravines, the walls of Babylon reached the tremendous height Herodotus describes.

The walls were made of bricks formed from clay and earth, which was dug from a trench that served as a moat once the wall was completed. These trenches were filled with water from the canals and were lined with the same bricks. For all this building they used cement made from a type of bitumen, a sticky oil which floated down a nearby river in great quantities.

The River Euphrates itself flowed through the city. There was a low wall along the banks of it, with openings at the ends of the streets and flights of steps going down to the water. These openings were blocked by gates of brass to prevent enemies from entering the city through the river. The great streets which ran all the way from the river to the outer walls were themselves crossed at right angles by other streets. In the outer walls, at the ends of all these streets, were massive gates of brass—a hundred in all. They were guarded from above by watchtowers, both inside and outside the wall. The wall itself was so broad that there was room between these watchtowers for a chariot pulled by four horses to drive and turn around.

The river divided the city into two parts. The king's palace was in the center of one of these divisions, surrounded by a vast circular wall which contained the palace, courts, parks, and gardens. In the center of the other part of the city was another enclosure which contained the temple of Belus. There was a high tower, made of eight separate towers stacked on top of each other with a staircase winding to the summit. On an upper story was a sort of chapel with a couch, table, and other gold furniture, all used for sacred rituals. And on the highest story of all was an observatory from which the Babylonian astrologers used to observe the heavens.

There was a bridge over the river and it was said that there was an underground passage under the river also, which was used for private communication between two citadels located on either end of the great bridge. All these buildings had a grand and imposing appearance and were decorated with a great variety of sculptures: animals, men, great kings, hunting scenes, battle scenes, and great events from Babylonian history.

The most remarkable of all the wonders of Babylon—though it may not have been built until after Cyrus' time—was the hanging gardens. Although called the hanging gardens, they were supported by arches built upon high terraces which could be reached by broad flights of steps. The terraces were surrounded by a wall twenty-five feet thick which also supported the arches. The whole structure thus formed a sort of square hill, rising to a broad, level area on top. This top level was four hundred feet long on each side.

The foundation of the gardens was built in this way: over the arches were laid broad flat stones, sixteen feet long and four feet wide. Over these was placed a layer of reeds and bitumen, and then another level of bricks, cemented carefully so as to be waterproof. This brick flooring was also covered with overlapping sheets of lead so that any water would run to the sides of the garden. Dirt was placed upon this surface, deep enough for large trees to take root and grow. There was a device built in the middle of the upper terrace which could draw water up from the river and distribute it throughout the garden.

The gardens were overflowing with every species of tree, plant, and vine which could produce fruit or flowers.

Every country in communication with Babylon contributed something to the endless variety of floral beauty. Highly experienced gardeners were constantly pruning the trees and vines, maintaining the walks, and planting new varieties. In a word, the hanging gardens of Babylon became one of the wonders of the world.

The country around Babylon was level and low all along the river and prone to flooding. A former queen named Nitocris had planned the construction of a large lake to catch the flood waters if the river overflowed. She also dug many channels for the river and used the dirt to raise the banks, creating levees, like those that are used to hold back the Mississippi at New Orleans. Nitocris' goal was two-fold. First, she wanted to open as many useful channels as she could in order to control the river. Second, she wanted to make navigation as complicated as possible in order to confuse foreign enemies trying to find their way to the capital. These were the rivers of Babylon where the captive Jews sat down and wept when they remembered Zion.

This queen Nitocris seems to have been quite famous for her engineering and architecture. It was she who built the bridge over the Euphrates within the city, and as there was jealousy and ill will between the two sides of the city, she had built a drawbridge so that the two sides could be easily separated. This drawbridge was generally up at night and down by day.

Herodotus relates a curious story about this queen, which, if true, further demonstrates the same originality and cleverness which characterized everything she did. She had her tomb built over one of the main gates of the city with the following inscription: "If any of my successors be in great need of money, let him open my tomb and take what he thinks proper, but only if the urgency is extreme."

The tomb remained undisturbed for some time after the queen's death, and the people began to avoid this gate altogether because of the dead body buried above. In time, a king needing money opened the tomb. He found no money inside, but only the dead body of the queen and another inscription: "If your greed were not as unquenchable as it is evil, you would not have intruded on the tomb of the dead."

It is not surprising that Cyrus, having been successful in all his wars so far, should now begin to feel a desire to bring Babylon under his sway. First, however, he had to secure his new lands in Lydia. He spent some time arranging his new government at Sardis and left portions of his army in the conquered cities there. He appointed Persians to command these forces, but as he wished to reconcile with the Lydians, he appointed many local officials to the new government. There seemed to be no danger in doing this, as the army was still commanded by Persians.

The most important of these city officials was the grand treasurer, who oversaw all the gold and silver in Sardis. Cyrus placed a Lydian named Pactyas in this position, hoping to please the Lydian people and make them more willing to submit to his authority. He then set out with the main army to return to the East, taking Croesus with him.

As soon as Cyrus had left Lydia, Pactyas encouraged the Lydians to revolt. He raised an army of Lydians and foreign mercenaries, hired with the treasures Cyrus had put in his charge. He then took possession of Sardis and locked up the Persian troops in the citadel.

When Cyrus heard this, he became very angry and determined to destroy the city. Croesus, however, inter-

The Conquest of Bablyon

ceded on its behalf. He recommended that Cyrus instead only disarm the population, and then pass laws that would turn the people towards habits of luxury and pleasure. "In a short time," said Croesus, "the people will become so effeminate that you will have nothing to fear from them."

Cyrus agreed with this plan. He sent a Median officer named Mazares at the head of a strong force, with orders to free the Persian soldiers and kill all the leaders of the rebellion except Pactyas. Pactyas was to be sent as a prisoner to Cyrus in Persia.

Pactyas did not wait for the arrival of Mazares. As soon as he heard of his approach, he abandoned the city and fled north to the city of Cyme, where he sought refuge. When Mazares had reached Sardis and re-established the government of Cyrus there, he sent messengers to Cyme, demanding the surrender of the fugitive.

The people of Cyme were uncertain whether they should comply. They said that they must first consult a very ancient and famous oracle near Miletus. They sent messengers to this oracle, asking if it was the will of the gods that Pactyas be handed over to Mazares. The answer was that they should hand him over.

They were preparing to do this when a prominent citizen named Aristodicus said that he was not satisfied with the oracle's reply. Surely the oracle would not counsel them to surrender a helpless fugitive to his enemies. The messengers must have misunderstood. He finally persuaded his countrymen to send a second group of messengers led by himself. On their arrival, Aristodicus addressed the oracle as follows: "To avoid a cruel death from the Persians, Pactyas, a Lydian, fled to us for refuge. The Persians demanded that we should surrender him. We are afraid of their power, but we are more afraid to hand over a helpless man asking for our protection without clear instructions from you to do so."

They received the same reply as before.

Still Aristodicus was not satisfied and so he began to make his way through the grove around the temple and destroy the nests which the birds had built there. This had the desired effect. A solemn voice came from inside the temple, saying: "Impious man! How dare you harm those who have placed themselves under my protection?"

Aristodicus asked the oracle why it watched over and guarded those who had sought its protection, while it directed the people of Cyme to abandon those who had sought theirs. To this the oracle answered: "I direct them to do it in order that such impious men may sooner bring down the judgment of heaven for having dared consider even the thought of betraying a helpless fugitive."

When this answer was reported to the people of Cyme, they did not dare give Pactyas, nor did they dare incur the enmity of the Persians by keeping and protecting him. So they sent him away secretly. The messengers of Mazares, however, followed him constantly, demanding him from every city where he took refuge, until they finally convinced one city to turn him over—partly by threats and partly by a reward. Mazares sent Pactyas as a prisoner to Cyrus. Soon after this, Mazares died and Harpagus was made governor of Lydia in his place.

Meanwhile Cyrus went on with his conquests in the heart of Asia until after a few years he had prepared for the attack of Babylon. He advanced with a large force to the city. The King of Babylon, whose name was Belshazzar, withdrew within the walls, shut the gates, and felt perfectly secure. A simple wall was a very effective protection as long as it was high enough so that it could not be climbed and thick enough to resist a battering ram, and Belshazzar knew his walls could withstand such attacks indefinitely. Therefore, once he had placed soldiers on the walls and in the watch towers, Belshazzar and his nobles simply gave themselves up to feasting in their palaces and gardens, for they felt perfectly secure and were abundantly supplied with the best food and drink from across the empire.

Cyrus advanced to the city. He stationed one large detachment of troops at the opening in the walls where the river entered the city, and another detachment below, where the river left the city. He then employed a vast force of laborers to dig new channels and to widen the existing ones. Waiting until night fall, Cyrus opened these canals so that they drew water out of the river until it ceased to flow into the city. The two detachments of troops then simply marched into Babylon through the dry stream bed. Belshazzar was in the middle of one of his feasts when it was announced to him that the Persians had taken complete possession of the city. He was, needless to say, thunderstruck.

CHAPTER IX

THE RESTORATION OF THE JEWS.

CYRUS' invasion of Babylonia and capture of the city occurred while the Jews were in captivity there. As a result, Cyrus is more connected with sacred history than any other great conqueror of ancient times.

It was a common custom in the ancient world for powerful rulers to take a conquered people captive and to use them as slaves. They employed them to some extent as household servants, but for the most part these slaves worked the land as agricultural laborers.

An account of the Jews' captivity in Babylon is given briefly in the final chapters of the book of 2nd Chronicles, and a more detailed description can be found in the book of Jeremiah. Jeremiah was a prophet who lived in the time of the captivity. Nebuchadnezzar, the king of Babylon, made repeated invasions into Judea, sometimes carrying off the reigning monarch, sometimes replacing him, sometimes taxing the land, and sometimes plundering the city of all the gold and silver he could find. Thus the Jews remained in a state of continual anxiety and terror for many years. King Zedekiah was the last of this oppressed and unhappy line of Jewish kings.

The prophet Jeremiah frequently denounced the sins of Jewish nation, declaring publicly that these terrible calamities were the judgments of Heaven and that worse punishments were coming. The people were distressed by these prophetic warnings, and some became very angry at Jeremiah. On one occasion, he stood in one of the public courts of the Temple and declared to the priests and people there that unless the nation repented of their sins and turned to God, the whole city would fall. Even the Temple itself would be destroyed and its site abandoned.

The priests and people, being exasperated with Jeremiah, seized him and brought before an assembly for trial. The judges asked him why he uttered such predictions and declared that he was behaving like an enemy to his country and deserved to die. Indeed, the people could hardly be restrained from open violence against him.

But Jeremiah remained calm and replied to their accusation like this: "Everything which I have said against this city and this Temple I have said by the direction of the Lord Jehovah. Instead of being angry with me for delivering my messages, you should look at your sins and repent of them. It may be that God will then have mercy upon you and avert the calamities which will otherwise most certainly come. As for myself, I am in your hands. Deal with me as you think best. You can kill me if you like, but it will only bring the guilt of shedding innocent blood upon yourselves and this city. I have said nothing but by the commandment of the Lord."

The Restoration of the Jews

The speech produced, as might be expected, great division among the hearers. Some were angrier than ever. Others defended him and insisted that he should not be killed. These won out for the moment, and Jeremiah was set free to continue his terrible announcements of the people's sins and the coming ruin of the city.

These truths were unwelcome, and soon other prophets began to appear with contrary predictions, quickly becoming popular for their promises of returning peace and prosperity. One of these false prophets was named Hananiah. On one occasion, Jeremiah made a small wooden yoke to symbolize to the people the bondage which he was predicting. Hananiah took this yoke and broke it, saying that, as he had broken Jeremiah's yoke, so God would break the yoke of Nebuchadnezzar within two years. Jeremiah replied that though the wooden yoke was broken, God would make for Nebuchadnezzar a yoke of iron with which he would place the Jews in bondage crueler than ever. Still, Jeremiah predicted that after seventy years of captivity the Jews should once again be restored to their native land.

He expressed this restoration of the Jews on one occasion through a sort of symbol. There was a piece of land in the country of the tribe of Benjamin which belonged to Jeremiah's family. At a time when Jeremiah was in prison, his nephew came to the prison and proposed that Jeremiah buy the land. Jeremiah agreed and did so in a very public manner. Title deeds were drawn up, witnesses were summoned, money was weighed and paid over, and the whole transaction was completed according to the normal procedures. Jeremiah then gave the papers to his scribe, directing him to put them somewhere safe, for after a period of time the country of Judea would be restored to the peaceful possession of the Jews, and all such titles to land would once more possess their original value.

On one occasion, while Jeremiah was imprisoned, he had to dictate his prophetic warnings to Baruch his scribe, because he could not proclaim them publicly. Baruch was instructed to read the scroll during a great festival, when all the people of Judea were gathered together. So he stationed himself near the entrance to the Temple, and calling upon the people to listen, he began to read. A great crowd gathered around. One of the bystanders went down to the king's palace and reported to the council that Baruch was reading one of Jeremiah's prophecies to a great crowd at the Temple. The council summoned Baruch to come immediately and to bring the prophecy with him.

When Baruch arrived, they had him read what he had written and asked where it came from. Baruch replied that he had written it word for word from Jeremiah's dictation. The council told him that they were obligated to report this to the king and that Jeremiah should hide in case the king became angry and tried to hurt him.

The council then reported these facts to the king, who sent one of his attendants, Jehudi, to bring him the scroll and read it to him. Jehudi did so, standing by a fire in the king's home, for it was very cold.

After Jehudi had read a few pages, the king, finding that it contained old denunciations and warnings which had angered him in the past, began to cut the parchment in pieces with a knife and throw it into the fire. Some standing by begged the king not to burn the scroll, but the king did not listen and sent officers to find Jeremiah and Baruch, but they were nowhere to be found.

Once the prophet became greatly distressed by the persecution which his warnings brought him. It was at a time when the Chaldean armies had been driven away from Jerusalem for a short period by the Egyptians, as one vulture drives away another from its prey. Jeremiah determined to take the opportunity to go to the province of Benjamin to visit his friends and family there. He was stopped at one of the gates and accused of planning to escape the city and desert to the Babylonians. The prophet denied the charge, but they ignored him and sent him back to Jerusalem, where the king's officers had him confined in a house they used as a prison.

After he had been imprisoned here for several days, the king had him brought to the palace and asked whether he had any prophecy from the Lord. Jeremiah replied that the word of the Lord was that the Babylonians would return and that King Zedekiah himself should fall into their hands and be taken captive to Babylon. He also asked that the king not send him back to the house where he had been imprisoned. The king agreed and had him sent to the public prison instead, where his confinement would not be as harsh, and ordered that the prophet continue to be given food as long as there was any left in the city.

But Jeremiah's enemies were not done. After a while they came again to the king and told him that the prophet had discouraged and weakened the people with his gloomy predictions and ought to be regarded as a public enemy. The king replied that he would turn Jeremiah over to them and they could do with him as they wished.

There was a dungeon in the prison which was only accessible from above. Prisoners were let down into it with ropes and left there to die of hunger. The bottom of it was wet and miry and Jeremiah, when lowered into it, sank into the deep mud. Here he soon would have died of hunger and misery, but the king felt guilty for what he had done and was worried that he might have delivered a true prophet of God into the hands of his enemies. When a slave named Ebed-Melech informed him that Jeremiah had been imprisoned in this pit, he immediately sent officers to remove him from the dungeon. The officers went and opened the prison. Letting down ropes and cloths, they called down to Jeremiah to place the cloths under his arms and then the ropes. He did so and they pulled him up safely out of the pit.

These cruel persecutions of the faithful prophet all failed to either silence him or avert the disasters which he predicted. At the chosen time, the foretold judgments all came to pass. The Babylonians invaded in force and encamped around the city. The siege lasted two years, until they ran out of food. Then King Zedekiah organized as strong a force as he could and tried to escape the city, leaving the city to its fate. He managed to make it through the Babylonian lines, but then he was chased down and captured. The city was then stormed and given up to plunder and destruction. Vast numbers of the inhabitants were killed and many more were taken captive. The important buildings were burned, the walls were broken down, and all the Jews' treasure was carried away to Babylon, including the gold and silver dishes used in the Temple. All this was seventy years before Cyrus' conquest of Babylon.

Of course, the deportation of a whole people to a foreign land is impossible, and a large number of Jews remained in Judea during the period of this captivity. Those that were carried away remained in miserable bondage for two generations. Some worked as agricultural laborers in the country around Babylon; others remained as servants in the city itself. The prophet Daniel lived in the palaces of the king. He was summoned to Belshazzar's feast on the same night that Cyrus captured the city to interpret the mysterious writing on the wall which announced the fall of the Babylonian monarchy.

One year after Cyrus had conquered Babylon, he issued an edict allowing the Jews to return to Jerusalem to rebuild the city and the Temple. This event had been long predicted by the prophets. We should not expect a conqueror like Cyrus to have any real interest in fulfilling the will of God, but he still acknowledged the supremacy of Jehovah in the proclamation and claimed to have been charged by God with the restoration of the Temple. It is believed by some scholars that Cyrus' true goal was to reestablish the Jewish nation as a barrier between himself and the Egyptians, who had long been deadly enemies of the Babylonians.

Whatever Cyrus' motives may have been, he decided to allow the Hebrew captives to return and issued a proclamation to that effect. As seventy years had passed since the beginning of their captivity, about two generations had died, and there could have been very few living who had ever seen the land of their fathers. However, the Jews were all eager to return. When they had assembled together with all their valuables, baggage, and provisions, a census was taken, and there were found to be forty-nine thousand six hundred and ninety-seven of them in all.

They also had seven or eight hundred horses, about two hundred and fifty mules, and about five hundred camels. Most of their baggage was carried by nearly seven thousand donkeys. The march of this peaceful multitude of families—men, women, and children together—all burdened with provisions and tools for honest work, must have been one of the greatest sights the world has ever seen.

The grand caravan made its long and difficult march from Babylon to Jerusalem without harm. All arrived safely and the people immediately began repairing the city walls and rebuilding the Temple. When at last the foundations of the Temple were laid, a great celebration was held to commemorate the event. This celebration involved a remarkable combination of rejoicing and mourning.

The younger part of the population, who had never seen Jerusalem in its former grandeur, felt only excitement at being re-established in the city of their fathers. The work of raising the Temple, whose foundations they had laid, was simply a new task which they looked forward to, whereas the old men who remembered the former Temple were filled with sad memories of their peaceful childhoods and the glory of the old Temple, which they knew would never be achieved again. It was customary in those days to express sorrow through cries and exclamations, and on this occasion, the cries of grief and regret were mingled with the shouts of rejoicing from the young, who knew nothing of the past and only looked forward to the future with hope.

The Jews met with significant opposition in their attempt to reconstruct their ancient city and to re-establish the worship of God there, as is told in detail in the books of Ezra and Nehemiah, but we must return now to the history of Cyrus.

CHAPTER X

THE STORY OF PANTHEA.

IN earlier chapters we have mainly followed the account of Herodotus, except in the story of Cyrus' childhood visit to his grandfather, which is taken from Xenophon. In this chapter, I shall tell the story of Panthea, which is also one of Xenophon's tales. I include it as yet another specimen of the romantic narratives which are common in Xenophon's history and also for the many examples it provides of ancient manners and customs. It is up to the reader to decide whether or not to view it as true history. We relate the story here in our own language, but the facts are all drawn faithfully from Xenophon's telling of it.

Panthea was one of many captives taken after Cyrus fought a great battle with the Assyrians. Her husband was an Assyrian general, though he himself was not captured with his wife. In addition to the prisoners, Cyrus' army also gathered a great deal of valuable plunder, including beautiful suits of armor, large sums of money, gold and silver dishes, and slaves—some prized for their beauty and others for their talents. Cyrus ordered these spoils to be distributed generously and evenly among his officers and soldiers, as he always did.

Among the prizes distributed to Cyrus were two famous singing women and Panthea. Cyrus thanked the distributors he had ordered to divide the plunder, but said that if anyone wanted either of his captives, they could have them. An officer asked for one of the singers and Cyrus was happy to give her away. As for Panthea, Cyrus had not yet seen her, but asked one of his close friends to look after her.

The name of this friend was Araspes, an officer. He was a Mede, and he had been a good friend of Cyrus when he was a boy visiting his grandfather in Media. The reader will perhaps remember that Araspes was mentioned as the special friend to whom Cyrus gave his robe when he returned to Persia.

When Araspes had received this charge, he asked Cyrus if he had himself seen the lady yet. Cyrus replied that he had not. Araspes then gave an account of her. Her husband's name was Abradates, and he was the king of Susa, though he was subordinate to the Assyrians. He had been away visiting another country at the time of the battle and thus had not been taken prisoner along with his wife.

Araspes went on to say that when they captured her, they had found her sitting in her tent with her serving ladies, patiently awaiting her doom. Despite the veils over their faces, there was something about Panthea which showed at once that she was the queen. The leader of Araspes' party asked them all to rise. They did so, and the extraordinary grace and beauty of Panthea became even clearer. She stood in a dejected posture, but her countenance, though sad, was inexpressibly lovely. She endeavored to appear calm and composed, though tears had obviously been falling from her eyes.

The soldiers pitied her, and their leader attempted to console her by telling her that she had nothing to fear and would have no reason to regret her capture, for they would find her a new husband just as good as her old one.

These well-meaning attempts at consolation did not appear to have the desired effect. The tears began to fall again, faster than before. She sobbed and cried aloud, tearing her robe in the customary expression of despair. Araspes said that part of her face was revealed in this and that she was the most beautiful woman he had ever seen. He wished Cyrus to see her.

Cyrus said no, he would not see her, lest he be captivated by her and lose his interest in the great military campaign he was in the middle of. Araspes replied that Cyrus should at least see her and would certainly be able to control himself from letting her distract him from his military duties. Cyrus said that it was not certain, and a long discussion followed between them. Araspes argued that every man had control of his own heart and could direct his feelings as he saw fit. Cyrus on the other hand maintained that human emotions were stronger than the human will and that no one could be sure of controlling the impulses of the heart—particularly when it came to love.

In the end, Cyrus jokingly advised Arasped to beware lest he prove that love was stronger than the will by becoming enamored with the queen himself. Araspes said that Cyrus need not fear; there was no danger of that. He took charge of the royal captive with a firm resolution to be faithful to Cyrus' trust, but as usually happens with those who are over-confident, Araspes failed when it finally came to the test.

He pitied the queen's misfortunes and admired the heroic patience with which she bore them. Her beauty and charm, which were only heightened by her sadness, touched his heart, and he began to take pleasure in granting her every wish. She was grateful and the few brief words with which she thanked him more than repaid him for his efforts. He began to find in her every movement an inexpressible charm until he became wholly absorbed by his interest in her. This was exactly what Cyrus had predicted. Araspes resolved many times to put these feelings aside, but whenever he returned into her presence these resolutions simply melted away, and he gladly let himself be controlled by his emotions.

Things continued in this way for some time. The army advanced from camp to camp with their captives behind them. New cities were taken, new provinces overrun, and new conquests planned. At last it happened that Cyrus needed a spy to send into a distant enemy's country, and it needed to be someone of high intelligence and rank, someone who could befriend the noblemen of that country—very different from the ordinary spy who merely reported the numbers of an enemy army. Cyrus did not know who to send.

In the meantime, Araspes had ventured to express his love to Panthea. She was offended, as she was faithful to her husband and felt that Araspes had betrayed Cyrus' trust. However, she did not rebuke him or complain to Cyrus. She simply turned him away, believing that if she did this firmly, Araspes would say no more. She was wrong. Araspes continued to bombard her with declarations of love, and finally she was forced to tell Cyrus.

Instead of being angry, Cyrus only laughed at Araspes' failure. He sent a messenger, warning Araspes to re-

The Story of Panthea

spect the feelings of such a woman as Panthea had proved herself to be. The messenger made the message much more severe than what Cyrus had actually dictated and harshly rebuked Araspes for harboring such impious feelings and betraying the sacred trust of his king. Araspes was overwhelmed with remorse and fear of punishment.

When Cyrus heard how his message had distressed Araspes, he sent for him. Araspes came. Cyrus told him not to worry. "I am not surprised," he said, "at what has happened. We all know how hard it is to resist the effect a beautiful woman has on our minds. Whatever wrong there has been should be considered as my fault, not yours, for I was wrong to place you in such temptation."

Araspes was astonished by Cyrus' generosity in taking the blame for himself and thanked him very earnestly for his kindness. News of his fault had spread through the army, and his enemies were predicting his disgrace while his friends advised him to escape before any worse calamity should befall him.

"If this is so," said Cyrus, "it puts you in a position to render me a great service." Cyrus then explained to Araspes how he needed a spy to send into their enemy's country. "You can pretend to run away," he said, "and it will be said that you fled for fear of my displeasure. I will pretend to have you pursued. The news of your escape will spread rapidly, so that when you arrive in the enemy's country they will be ready to accept you as a deserter from my army."

They agreed upon this plan, and Araspes prepared to depart. Cyrus gave him his instructions, and together they invented the fictitious information about Cyrus' situation and plans which he was to share with the enemy. When all was ready, Cyrus asked him how he was willing to thus leave the beautiful Panthea. Araspes replied that when he was absent from Panthea he was capable of making the decisions his duty required, while in her presence he found his love for her absolutely uncontrollable.

As soon as Araspes was gone, Panthea, who believed he really had fled in fear of the king's anger, sent a message to Cyrus expressing her regret at Araspes' desertion. She said she would gladly try to make up for his loss by sending for her own husband, who was discontent with the tyrannical king he served. "If you will allow me to send for him," she added, "I am sure he will come and join your army, and I assure you that you will find him a much more faithful servant than Araspes."

Cyrus agreed to this proposal, and Panthea sent for Abradates. Abradates came at the head of two thousand horse, which were a very valuable addition to Cyrus' forces. The reunion of Panthea and her husband was exceedingly joyful. When Abradates learned how honorably she had been treated by Cyrus, he was overwhelmed with gratitude and declared he would do everything in his power to repay the kindness.

Abradates began at once to plan how best his soldiers might serve Cyrus. He noticed that Cyrus was interested, at that time, in building a force of armed chariots. This was a very expensive force, for the chariots were heavy and strong and typically drawn by two horses. They had short, scythe-like steel blades projecting from the axle on each side, which would mow down the enemy as the chariots were driven among them. In addition to the driver of the horses, each chariot would also hold one or more heavily armed warriors who stood in the back and fought with javelins and spears. The great plains of that part of Asia were very well suited to this kind of warfare.

Abradates immediately had a hundred such chariots outfitted at his own expense and provided his own horses to draw them. He made one chariot much larger than the rest and drawn by eight horses, for he meant to command these chariots himself. His wife Panthea prepared a suit of gold armor from her own treasury, and brass armor for the horses. She also set aside a purple robe, a purple crest for the helmet, and gold arm bands, but she kept all these things secret until the day arrived when her husband was going into battle for the first time with his chariots. Then she brought them to his tent.

Abradates was astonished. When he realized that these things had come from his wife's personal treasury he exclaimed in surprise and pleasure, "And so, to provide me with this splendid armor you have been depriving yourself of all your finest and most beautiful ornaments!"

"No," said Panthea, "you are yourself my finest ornament and you will now appear in others' eyes as you do in mine."

Abradates' appearance was certainly splendid on this occasion. The whole chariot with its eight horses in their colorful trappings and splendid armor, and Abradates, standing inside in his armor of gold, presented a most imposing scene. Spectators thought he seemed most worthy to lead the column of a hundred such chariots, but so great was their admiration of Panthea's affection for her husband and so impressed were they with her beauty that they barely noticed the great chariot, resplendent horses, and golden warrior. Panthea stood for a while by the chariot, speaking quietly to Abradates, reminding him of their obligation to Cyrus for his noble treatment of her and urging him to be faithful, brave, and true in return.

The driver then closed the door to the chariot, separating Panthea from her husband, though she walked along after it as it drove off. Abradates turned and waved goodbye, saying, "Farewell, Panthea. Go back now to your tent and do not be anxious about me. Farewell." Panthea turned and let her attendants lead her away. The spectators turned too, watching her go, and no one paid any attention to the chariot or Abradates until she was gone.

As Cyrus passed along the battlefield, examining his troops before the fight, he paused to speak with Abradates and inspect the chariots. He saw that the chariots were drawn up in a part of the field where they faced a very formidable force of Egyptian soldiers who were allies of their enemy. Abradates descended from his chariot and conversed with Cyrus for a few moments to receive his last orders. Cyrus directed him not to attack the enemy until he had received a certain signal. At length Abradates returned to his chariot, and Cyrus moved on. Abradates then moved slowly along his lines, encouraging his men and giving them their last directions. All eyes were on the magnificent sight of his armor and chariot, and his eight horses stepping proudly, their bronze armor clanking.

When at last the signal was given, Abradates called on the other chariots to follow, and the whole line charged to attack the Egyptians. Properly trained war horses will fight with their hooves with as much reckless determination as men with spears. They rush madly at any opposition, striking down and leaping over whatever comes in their way. As Cyrus passed from one part of the battle to another, he saw the horses of Abradates' line dashing impetuously into the thickest ranks of the enemy. The men were beaten down on every side by the horses' hooves, or overturned by the wheels, or cut down by the scythes. And those who escaped were impaled by spears thrown from the chariots. The heavy wheels rolled mercilessly over the bodies of the fallen, while the scythes tore to pieces everything in their way. As Cyrus rode by he saw Abradates in the middle of this scene, driving on in his chariot, shouting to his men in a frenzy of excitement and triumph.

This battle was one of the greatest and most important which Cyrus fought. When at last his enemies were routed and driven from the field, the army drew back from the slaughter and camped for the night. The next day the generals came to Cyrus' tent to discuss the division of the spoils and the future movements of the army. Abradates was not there. At first, Cyrus did not notice his absence in all the excitement and confusion. When he asked about him, a soldier present told him that he had been killed from his chariot in the midst of the Egyptians and his wife was at that moment with the body on the banks a river that flowed near the field of battle. Cyrus uttered a loud exclamation of astonishment and sorrow. He left his business with the council and immediately rode off to find Panthea.

When he arrived at the spot, the dead body of Abradates was lying upon the ground with Panthea at its side, holding the head in her lap, overwhelmed with unspeakable sorrow. Cyrus leaped from his horse and knelt by the side of the corpse, saying, "Alas! Thou brave and faithful soul, art thou gone?"

He took hold of the hand of Abradates—and the arm came away from the body. It had been cut off by an Egyptian sword. Panthea's grief broke forth anew. She cried out in anguish, told Cyrus that the rest of the body was in the same condition, and replaced the arm in the position in which she had arranged it before. Her sobs and tears almost kept her from speaking. She bitterly cursed herself for having been the cause of her husband's death by urging him to fidelity and courage when he went into battle. "And now," she said, "he is dead, while I, who urged him forward into danger, am still alive."

Cyrus said what he could to console Panthea's grief, but without success. He gave orders for her to be given everything she needed and promised to provide for her in the future. "You shall be treated," he said, "while you remain with me, in the most honorable manner, or if you have any friends whom you wish to join, you shall be sent to them safely as soon as you wish."

Panthea thanked him for his kindness. She said she had a friend whom she wished to join, but meanwhile she wanted to be left alone with her servants and her dead husband. Cyrus withdrew. When he had gone, Panthea sent away the servants also, keeping only her waiting-maid. The waiting-maid began to be concerned at these mysterious arrangements and wondered what her mistress was going to do. Then Panthea produced a sword which she had hidden beneath her robe. The maid begged her with many tears not to kill herself, but Panthea was immovable. She said she could not live any longer. She instructed the maid to cover her body with the same cloak as her husband and to have them both placed in the same grave, and before the maid could do anything to save her, Panthea had laid down with her head on her husband's chest and stabbed herself. In a few minutes she was dead.

Cyrus expressed his respect for the memory of Abradates and Panthea by building a lofty monument over their common grave.

CHAPTER XI

CONVERSATIONS.

E have given the story of Panthea in our own language, but without any embellishment whatsoever. Each reader will judge for himself whether such a story, written for the entertainment of the public at games and celebrations, should be seen as invented romance or true history.

Many similar extraordinary adventures can be found in Xenophon's history. There are also many long and detailed conversations. If these conversations really happened, Xenophon would have required a great deal of skill to produce such accurate reports of them as he has given. The circumstances of these conversations are also worth investigating, for we can often tell whether they are situations which might occur in real life or whether they are invented to create the opportunity for the conversation. It was the custom in ancient days to try to add to a discussion by presenting various views as conversation arising from invented circumstances. We shall present in this chapter some examples these conversations.

Once, after Cyrus had won a great victory and was celebrating in the midst of his army with spectacles and games, he began a series of races, in which the various nations in his army entered their champions as competitors. The army marched out of the captured city in a magnificent procession with animals to be offered as sacrifices dressed in trappings of gold, horsemen in splendid war chariots, and banners of every kind. When the procession reached the race-ground, the spectators gathered around it and the racing began.

When it was the turn of the Sacian nation to enter the course, a private citizen of no rank emerged as the champion. Though the man was nobody, his horse was as fast as the wind. He flew around the arena with astonishing speed and finished while his opponent was still halfway around the course. Everybody was astonished. Cyrus asked the Sacian whether he would be willing to sell the horse if Cyrus gave him a kingdom for it—kingdoms being the currency emperors like Cyrus used to make their purchases. The Sacian replied that he would not sell his horse for any kingdom, but that he would readily give him away to a worthy man.

"Come with me," said Cyrus, "and I will show you where you may throw while blindfolded and not miss a worthy man."

Saying this, Cyrus took the Sacian to a part of the field where his officers were moving to and fro on their horses and chariots. The Sacian picked up a hard clod of earth.

"Throw!" said Cyrus.

The Sacian shut his eyes and threw.

It happened that an officer named Pheraulas was riding by at that instant, conveying some orders to another part of the field. Pheraulas had once been a poor man, but Cyrus had promoted him to a high position because of his great faithfulness and zeal. The Sacian's clod struck Pheraulas in the mouth and hurt him badly. It is the duty of a good soldier to stand at his post or carry out his orders as long as he is physically able, and Pheraulus rode on without even turning to see what had hit him.

The Sacian opened his eyes, looked around, and asked who it was that he had hit. Cyrus pointed to the horseman riding away, saying, "That is the man, who is riding so fast past those chariots yonder. You hit *him*."

"Why did he not turn back, then?" asked the Sacian.

"It is strange that he did not," said Cyrus. "He must be some kind of madman."

The Sacian went in pursuit of him. He found Pheraulas with his face covered with blood and dirt and asked him if he had received a blow. "I have," said Pheraulas, "as you can see." "Then," said the Sacian, "I give you my horse." Pheraulas asked why. So the Sacian told him about his conversation with Cyrus and said that he would gladly give Pheraulas his horse, as he proved himself to be a most worthy man.

Pheraulas accepted the gift with many thanks, and he and the Sacian became very good friends from then on.

Some time later, Pheraulas invited the Sacian to a magnificent feast at his splendid home, which was furnished with the most gorgeous carpets, canopies, and couches. The Sacian was very impressed by all this and asked Pheraulas if he had been a rich man at home before he joined Cyrus' army. Pheraulas replied that he had not. His father was a farmer, and he himself used to till the land with the other laborers. All the wealth and luxury which he now enjoyed had been given to him, he said, by Cyrus.

"How fortunate you are!" said the Sacian. "You must enjoy your present wealth all the more for having grown up in poverty."

"It is not so," replied Pheraulas, "for I cannot receive any more of our natural enjoyments than I could before. I cannot eat any more, drink any more, sleep any more, or do anything of these with any more pleasure than I did when I was poor. All I gain by wealth is that I have more to watch and more to take care of. I have many servants to provide for and who constantly need my help. One calls for food, another for clothes, another for a doctor. My other possessions are also a constant worry. A man tells me one day that a wolf has attacked my sheep; on another day, that my oxen have fallen from a cliff, or that a fight has broken out among my flocks or herds. My wealth, therefore, only increases my anxiety and trouble, without adding at all to my joys."

"But those must be unusual events," said the Sacian. "When things are going well, you can look around on all your possessions and remember that they are yours, and then certainly you must be happier than I am."

"It is true," said Pheraulas, "that there is a pleasure in the possession of wealth, but that pleasure is not great enough to balance out the calamities and losses that also come with it. The suffering of losing our possessions is greater than the pleasure of keeping them and even deprives men of sleep."

"That is true," replied the Sacian. "Men are not kept awake by the excitement of continuing to possess their wealth, but they often are when they first acquire it."

"Yes, indeed," replied Pheraulas, "and if the enjoyment of *being* rich could remain as great as the enjoyment of *becoming* rich, then the rich would be very happy men. But they who possess much, must lose much, and spend much, and give much."

The Sacian was not convinced. The giving and spending, he maintained, would be themselves a source of pleasure. He should like to have much for the very purpose of being able to give much away. Finally, since the Sacian seemed to think that riches would give him so much pleasure and since Pheraulas only found them to be a source of trouble, Pheraulas proposed that he give all his wealth to the Sacian, and that he himself only keep enough to live on.

"You are joking," said the Sacian.

"No," said Pheraulas, "I am serious." And he renewed his suggestion and pressed the Sacian urgently to accept it.

The Sacian said nothing would give him greater pleasure. He expressed great thanks, and promised to supply Pheraulas with the best of everything he might want. He also promised that he would convince Cyrus to let Pheraulas out of the army so that he might from then on live quietly and enjoy all the benefits of wealth without any of its responsibilities.

The plan was arranged and put into action. Both parties were extremely pleased with the result, and they lived thus together for a long time. Whatever Pheraulas gained in any way, he always brought to the Sacian, and the Sacian, by accepting it, relieved Pheraulas of all responsibility and care. The Sacian loved Pheraulas because he was always bringing him gifts, and Pheraulas loved the Sacian because he was always willing to accept the gifts.

Among the other conversations Xenophon records are samples of those which took place at feasts in Cyrus' tent when he had invited his officers to dine with him. Cyrus began one of these conversations by asking the officers whether they did not think that the common soldiers were equal to the officers in intelligence, courage, and military skill, and all the other qualities of a good soldier.

"I do not know how that could be," replied one of the officers. "I cannot tell how they will prove when we meet the enemy, but I have never known a set of fellows more obstinate and rude than those in my regiment. The other day, when there had been a sacrifice, the meat was sent around to be distributed among the soldiers, beginning at one end of the line and continuing back and forth. One man did not get as much as the others, and he immediately broke out in loud and angry complaints, declaring that this method of division was unfair.

"At this," continued the officer, "I called to the man and invited him to stand by me down at the beginning of the line, where he might have a better chance at receiving a good share. He did so. It happened that the next distribution began at the other end, and so we were last. This man, believing that only the smallest pieces of meat were left, began to complain even more than before. 'Be patient,' said I. 'Soon enough they will begin with us, and then you will have the best chance of all.' And so it proved. The next distribution began with us and the man took his share first. But when the second and third men took theirs, he fancied that their pieces look larger than his, and he put his meat back, intending to take a bigger one—but the steward with the meat moved on quickly, so that the man lost his food altogether. He was then quite furious with rage and frustration."

Cyrus and all the officers laughed heartily at this story of greediness and discontent, and then a few other similar stories were told by other guests. One officer said that a few days earlier he had been drilling a squad of men whom he was teaching to march. When he gave the order, one man at the head of the squad marched forward, but all the rest stood still. "I asked him," said the officer, "what he was doing. 'Marching,' he said, 'as you ordered me to do.' 'It was not you alone that I ordered to march,' I said, 'but all.' So I sent him back to his place and gave the command again. Then they all advanced toward me in disorder, each on his own without paying any attention to the others, and leaving the file-leader behind altogether. The file-leader said, 'Keep back! Keep back!' At this the men were angry and asked who they were supposed to obey."

Cyrus and his guests were so amused by this story that the speaker was here interrupted by universal laughter.

"Finally," continued the officer, "I sent the men back to their places and explained to them that when a command was given, they were to obey it carefully and in order, each man following the one before him. 'You must all imitate the action of the file-leader,' I said. 'When he advances, you advance, following him in a line.' Just at this moment," the officer went on, "a man came to me for a letter which he was going to deliver to Persia. I told the file-leader to run to my tent and bring the letter to me. He immediately set off. The rest of the soldiers obeyed literally the directions I had just given them and followed him, all twenty men running across the field in a line to fetch a letter!"

When the laughter had ended, Cyrus said he thought his officers could not complain about their soldiers, for according to these stories they certainly seemed ready to obey. At this, one of the guests, a gloomy man named

Aglaitadas who had not joined in the laughter, asked Cyrus if he believed the stories to be true.

"Why?" asked Cyrus. "What do *you* think of them?"

"*I* think," said Aglaitadas, "that these officers invented them to make the company laugh. It is clear that they were not telling the truth, since they told the stories in such a proud and arrogant way."

"Arrogant!" said Cyrus. "You cannot call them arrogant. Even if they invented these stories, it was not for selfish reasons, but only to amuse us. Such people should be called polite and agreeable, not arrogant."

"Aglaitadas," said one of the officers, "if we had told you melancholy stories to make you gloomy, then you might have a reason to be upset but you cannot complain that we tried to make you merry!"

"Yes," said Aglaitadas, "I think I can. Making a man laugh is an insignificant and useless thing. It is far better to make him weep. The thoughts and the conversations that make us serious, thoughtful, and sad, and even move us to tears, are the best."

"Well," replied the officer, "if you take my advice, you will use all your power to inspire gloom and tears in our enemies, and give the mirth and laughter to us. There must be a great deal of laughter still inside you, for none ever comes out. You neither use it, nor do you allow our friends to."

"Then," said Aglaitadas, "why do you attempt to draw it from me?"

"It *is* absurd!" said another officer. "For one could more easily strike fire out of Aglaitadas than make him laugh!"

Aglaitadas could not help smiling at this. Cyrus, with an air of feigned seriousness, reproved the man who had spoken for corrupting the most sensible man in the company by making him smile.

These examples give a clearer idea of the Cyropaedia of Xenophon than any general description could. The book is a drama, made up of narratives like the story of Panthea, and conversations like those contained in this chapter—all mixed with long discussions on the principles of government and the management of armies. These principles are no longer applicable, for the circumstances of the world have changed, and yet the book remains valuable as a simple and beautiful example of the language in which it is written—which, however, cannot be appreciated except by those who read it in the original Greek.

CHAPTER XII

THE DEATH OF CYRUS.

AFTER having conquered the Babylonian empire, Cyrus found himself the ruler of nearly all of known Asia. It was believed that beyond his dominions lay vast tracts of desolate uninhabitable territory—lands of excessive heat, lands of excessive cold, barren deserts, incessant rains, or even swamps. To the north was the great unexplored Caspian Sea, which they believed extended as far north as the Arctic Ocean.

On the west side of the Caspian Sea were the Caucasian Mountains, which were believed to be the highest on the globe. Near these mountains there was a country inhabited by a wild people called the Scythians. This was a sort of generic term which was used in those days to mean almost all of the native tribes beyond the borders of civilization. The Scythians who lived on the borders of the Caspian Sea, however, were not completely uncivilized. They possessed many of the early technologies which are first to develop in warlike nations. They had no iron or steel, but they were accustomed to work with other metals, particularly gold and brass. They tipped their spears and javelins with brass and made armor of brass plates, both for themselves and their horses. They also made many ornaments of gold, which they attached to their helmets, their belts, and their banners. They were fearsome warriors, being reckless in battle like all other northern nations. Their armies contained great bodies of cavalry, for they were excellent horsemen and had many horses to practice with.

The various conquests through which Cyrus gained possession of his extensive dominions took about thirty years. It was near the end of his life that he formed a plan to invade these wild northern regions, hoping to add them to his kingdom.

He had two sons, Cambyses and Smerdis. His wife is said to have been a daughter of Astyages, whom he married soon after his conquest of Media in order to pacify the country by making a Median princess his queen. Among the western nations of Europe such a marriage would be forbidden, since Astyages was Cyrus' grandfather, but among the Orientals, such marriages were not uncommon in those days. It would seem that this queen was not living at the time of the events in this chapter. Her sons had grown up and were now princes of great importance.

One of the Scythian or northern tribes was called the Massagetae, and they had an extensive and powerful realm. They were ruled at this time by a queen named Tomyris. She was an aging widow. She had an adult son named Spargapizes who was heir to the throne and commander-in-chief of her armies.

Cyrus' first plan for adding the realm of Massagetae to his own empire was by a matrimonial alliance. He raised an army and marched north, sending ambassadors ahead with offers of marriage to the queen. The queen knew very well that it was her lands that attracted Cyrus and not herself. She refused the offers and sent back word forbidding Cyrus to enter her realm.

Cyrus, however, continued to approach. The boundary between his dominions and hers was at the River Araxes, a stream flowing from west to east, through the central parts of Asia towards the Caspian Sea. As Cyrus advanced, he found the country growing more and more wild and desolate. It was inhabited by savage tribes who lived on roots and herbs and had a very strange custom. There was a plant whose fruit gave off strong fumes when roasted on a fire and produced an effect like alcohol. These savages, Herodotus says, would gather around a fire during their festivities and throw some of this fruit into it. When the fruit's fumes began to intoxicate the circle, they would throw on more fruit, becoming more and more excited until they would jump up, dance, and sing in a state of complete intoxication.

Among savages such as these and through the forests and wildernesses, Cyrus advanced till he reached the Araxes. Here, after much thought, he determined to build a floating bridge using boats and rafts from the natives. It would obviously be easier to use these boats to simply float the men across the river, rather than building a bridge out of them, but it would also be slower and more dangerous. And if they were attacked while part of the army was floating across, they would almost certainly be defeated. Cyrus therefore planned the construction of a bridge as a way of moving his army across in a single body that could be formed into battle order without delay.

While Cyrus was busy building the bridge, ambassadors appeared, sent by Tomyris to warn Cyrus not to invade her kingdom. She reminded him that he could not foresee the result. Fortune had favored him thus far, it was true, but fortune might change, and he might suddenly find himself at the end of his victories. Still, she said, she did not expect that he would listen to this warning, and she did not object to him continuing his invasion, for she did not fear him. She would even withdraw her forces three days' march so that he might cross the river safely, without having to build a bridge, or, if he preferred, she would cross the river and meet him on his own side, in which case he must pull back three days' march. She would then march to attack him.

Cyrus called a council of war to consider this choice. He laid the question before his officers and generals and asked for their opinion. They all agreed it would be best for him to take the second choice.

There was, however, one person at the council who gave Cyrus different advice. This was Croesus, the fallen king of Lydia. Ever since his capture, he had remained in the camp and household of Cyrus and had often accompanied him in his expeditions. Though a captive, he seems to have been a friend, and he often appears in history as a wise and honest counselor to Cyrus. He was present on this occasion, and he disagreed with the opinion of the officers.

"I should apologize, perhaps," he said, "for presuming to offer any counsel, captive as I am, but I have been taught some wisdom in the school of calamity and misfortune which you have never had the opportunity to learn. It seems to me much better for you to not fall back, but to advance and attack Tomyris in her own dominions. If you fall back and then Tomyris defeats you in battle, then she is already three days' march into your dominions and could invade further before you can raise another army. But even if you defeat her instead, then you will be six days' march behind where you could be if you advance now.

"I propose the following plan: cross the river according to Tomyris' offer and advance three days' journey into her country. Leave a small part of your force there with your most valuable baggage and supplies—such things that the enemy would be most likely to plunder. Then fall back with the main body of your army secretly toward the river, and encamp in an ambush. The enemy will defeat your advance force. Believing your whole army to be vanquished, they will seize the plunder in disorder and the discipline of their army will be overthrown. They will begin feasting on the provisions and drinking the wines, and then you may attack suddenly with the rest of your army and overwhelm them while they are in the middle of their revelry."

Cyrus decided to adopt Croesus' plan. He told Tomyris' ambassadors that he would take the first choice. If she would draw back three days' march from the river, he would cross with his army and attack her as soon as possible. The ambassadors delivered this message to their queen, and she drew back to the appointed place and left her forces to wait under the command of her son.

Cyrus seems to have felt some foreboding about this expedition. He was old and not as able as he once was to endure the hardships of such campaigns. Furthermore, they were advancing into a remote, wild, and dangerous country, and he must have been aware that he might not return. Perhaps he also felt some guilt at thus invading an innocent neighbor. Whatever the case, he chose to settle the affairs of his government before he set out in order to maintain peace while he was gone and to ensure the safe transfer of power to his heir in case he never return.

Accordingly, in front of his whole army, he made his son Cambyses regent of the realm during his absence. He ordered Cambyses to pay Croesus every honor, attention, and care, and arranged for the two of them to return to the capital with the large number of attendants that had followed the camp thus far. These arrangements being complete, Cyrus took leave of his son and of Croesus, crossed the river with his army, and began the march.

The uneasiness which Cyrus seems to have felt on this memorable march affected even his dreams. It seems there was among his officers a certain general named Hystaspes. He had a son named Darius, about twenty years old, who had been left at home in Persia since he was not old enough to accompany the army. One night, immediately after crossing the river, Cyrus dreamed that he saw this young Darius with wings on his shoulders that overshadowed the world—one wing over Asia and one wing over Europe. When Cyrus awoke and considered this dream, it seemed to him to indicate that Darius was plotting to rule his empire. He took it as a warning.

In the morning, he sent for Hystaspes and told him the dream. "I have no doubt," said Cyrus, "that it means your son is planning an ambitious treason. Return home, stop him, and let him be ready to give me an account of his conduct when I come back."

Having received these orders, Hystaspes left the army and returned to Persia. The name of this Hystaspes eventually acquired immortality in a singular way. In later years Darius did gain very extended power and became Darius the Great. However, as there were several other Persian monarchs called Darius, it gradually became customary to call him Darius Hystaspes, and thus the name of the father has become familiar to all mankind.

The Death of Cyrus

After sending Hystaspes off, Cyrus marched on. He followed Croesus' plan in all respects. He marched his army into Tomyris' country to the agreed upon point. Here he left a weak portion of his army, with great supplies of food and wine and valuables. He then drew back with the main body of his army toward the Araxes and concealed his forces. The result was just as Croesus had expected. The weak group of soldiers left behind was attacked and routed by Tomyris' troops. The provisions fell into the hands of the victors and soon their whole camp was consumed with wild celebration. Even the commander, Spargapizes, Tomyris' son, became drunk with wine.

While this was happening, the main body of Cyrus' army suddenly fell upon them. The provisions and valuables were recovered, large numbers of the enemy were slain, and many more taken prisoner—including Spargapizes. His hands were bound, and he was placed under heavy guard in Cyrus camp.

This triumphantly successful strategy would have made Cyrus master of the whole realm, if it had actually been Tomyris' whole force that they had defeated, as they believed. It seems that Tomyris had learned by scouts and spies how large a force Cyrus had, and had only sent a detachment of her own troops to attack them, so that two thirds of her army still remained untouched. She would have no doubt attacked immediately, had it not been for her maternal concern for her captive son. She did not know what cruelties he would suffer if she were to anger Cyrus now. So while her heart was burning with anger and a thirst for revenge, her hand was restrained. She kept back her army and sent Cyrus a message of peace.

She told Cyrus that it had only been one third of her forces that he had defeated, and that with the remainder she held him completely in her power. She urged him to be satisfied with the damage he had already done, and to free her son and retreat from her kingdom. If he would do so, she would allow him to depart in peace, but if he would not, she swore by the great sun god of her people that she would drown Cyrus in blood.

Of course Cyrus was not frightened by such threats. He refused to free the captive prince or to withdraw from the country, and both sides began to prepare for war.

Spargapizes was drunk when he was taken and unaware of the calamity which had befallen him. When he finally awoke from his stupor and learned the full extent of his misfortune and disgrace, he was overwhelmed with astonishment and shame. The more he thought about it, the more hopeless things seemed. Even if he survived, he would never regain his honor. He begged Cyrus to allow him at least liberty within the camp. Cyrus, perhaps pitying his distress, agreed. Spargapizes waited until he was unguarded and then seized a weapon and killed himself.

His mother Tomyris was frantic with grief and rage when she heard this. She now considered Cyrus not only the destroyer of her kingdom's peace, but also the murderer of her son. Without a reason to restrain her thirst for revenge any longer, she began to gather all the additional troops she could from every corner of her kingdom. Cyrus also began to strengthen his lines and to prepare for the great final struggle.

At length the armies approached each other, and the battle began. The archers attacked first with showers of arrows as the armies advanced. When the arrows were gone, the men fought hand to hand with spears and swords. The Persians fought desperately, for they were fighting for their lives. They were deep in enemy country with all possibility of retreat cut off by the broad river behind them, and they were fighting a wild foe whose natural savagery was only increased by the anger of their queen. For a long time, it was unclear which side was winning. Neither side would retreat or surrender, and though all their comrades fell, the survivors continued to fight until they were all slain. It finally became clear that the Scythians were winning, and when night came, the Persian army was found to be almost entirely destroyed. The Scythians found the dead body of Cyrus among the mutilated remains which covered the battlefield, and they carried it to Tomyris in ferocious joy and triumph.

Tomyris treated the corpse with every possible insult and indignity, mutilating it as if it could still feel the injuries. "Miserable wretch!" she cried. "Though I am in the end your conqueror, you have ruined my peace and happiness forever. You have murdered my son. But I promised you your fill of blood, and you shall have it!" So saying, she filled a jar with the blood of her Persian captives, cut off Cyrus' head, and threw it into the jar, exclaiming, "Drink, insatiable monster, till your murderous thirst is quenched!"

This was the end of Cyrus. Cambyses, his son, whom he had made regent during his absence, succeeded without mishap to the throne of his vast dominions.

In considering this melancholy end to this great conqueror's story, our minds naturally go back to his childhood, and we wonder how such a gentle, generous boy should become so selfish and unfeeling as a man. But such are the inevitable effects of ambition and love of power. The history of a conqueror is always a tragic tale. He begins life with great and noble qualities, which always awaken in us the same admiration that his friends and countrymen felt for him. But he ends life neglected and hated. His ambition has been gratified, but has not brought peace or happiness. Instead it has only filled his soul with uneasiness, discontent, suspicion, and misery. Generosity and nobility seem to be necessary for the beginning of military success, and selfishness and cruelty seem to be the almost inevitable end of it. The exceptions to this rule, though splendid, are very few.

more from Canon Press

Cleopatra sent a message to Caesar, asking permission to appear before him and plead her own cause. Caesar agreed. She took a single boat, the smallest possible number of attendants, and sailed to Alexandria.

When they reached the city, they waited until night, and then advanced to the walls. Her servant Apollodorus rolled the queen up in a carpet and wrapped it in cloth, so that it looked like an ordinary package of merchandise. He then threw the load over his shoulder and entered the city. Cleopatra was about twenty-one years old, but she was slender and graceful, so the burden was not very heavy. At the gates of the palace, Apollodorus told the guards that he had a present for Caesar. They let him pass, and he carried his package safely to Caesar's quarters.

Caesar was charmed when it was unrolled to reveal Cleopatra.

CLEOPATRA
MAKERS OF HISTORY SERIES